The Worker Elite

Notes on the

"Labor Aristocracy"

BROMMA

KER
SPL
EBE
DEB
2014

The Worker Elite: Notes on the Labor Aristocracy
Kersplebedeb 2014

ISBN: 978-1-894946-57-5
First printing

Kersplebedeb Publishing & Distribution
CP 63560
CCCP Van Horne
Montreal, Quebec
Canada H3W 3H8
email: info@kersplebedeb.com
web: www.kersplebedeb.com
           www.leftwingbooks.net

Layout by Kersplebedeb

CONTENTS

AUTHOR'S PREFACE

I'M A MIDDLE CLASS PERSON. MY PARENTS STARTED *out without much money, but they quickly moved up the economic ladder. By the time I left elementary school, my family was comfortable financially. I had a privileged education, tailored for a life in the bubble of the intelligentsia.*

But that bubble made me claustrophobic. Starting as a teenager, I took a series of working class jobs to make extra money. I soon realized that those jobs were windows into a wider and more interesting world. Later, in the 1970s, I got caught up in radical politics. Older and wiser activists in the Movement drummed into me the pivotal role of the working class.

Eventually I decided to go "into the factories." I was part of a wave of young intellectuals in the US who were determined to commit class suicide. We were intent on helping make revolution from inside the working class. It's a decision I never regretted, even though it didn't work out quite the way I expected.

Since those early days I've had a bunch of industrial jobs. I've been part of lots of shop floor struggles, picket lines, job actions, strikes. I've tried to bring radical politics into my workplaces, and watched others do the same. I've seen left-wing caucuses and parties come and go. Most of my fellow "factory implanters" went back to graduate school or took union staff jobs years ago. The working class revolution we envisioned didn't happen.

But I never had any desire to relaunch life as a professional or academic, worthy as such a path can be. I didn't want a career in the labor bureaucracy. I liked working with my hands. I liked working in industry. And I mostly liked my co-workers.

Overall, I've been fortunate. I experienced some challenging situations, but I never got badly injured. I learned a lot, saw a lot, and joined forces with other workers to win some small victories against discrimination, unsafe conditions, and unfairness.

Now I'm retired, with a pension—something that only happens to privileged workers. I wouldn't say I ever made a full transformation from intellectual to working class person. That's a big change, socially, culturally, and psychologically. But through sheer longev-

ity I became more or less internal to the working class—part of working class life. Fellow workers sometimes guessed that I wasn't born working class. Or they found out when I told them. Still, there came a time when I'd been a worker longer than most of them had.

And, as I eventually figured out, there was something significant that I always had in common with my co-workers: We were all middle class.

We weren't doing stoop labor in the fields. We weren't leaving our children behind to work as domestics in a foreign land. We weren't leaning over a sewing machine in a garment sweatshop 12 hours a day. We were well-paid industrial workers in one of the wealthiest countries in the world; part of a relatively small privileged minority of the global workforce.

It took me a long time to accept the truth: that all my efforts at class suicide basically moved me sideways, from one middle class into another. Like I say, this has worked out fine for me personally. But becoming a middle class worker, and becoming part of the struggles of middle class workers, turned out to have very little to do with revolution. Revolution is something much harder.

These notes take a critical view of the role of the worker elite under capitalism. That doesn't mean I hate middle class workers. I'm one myself. I don't hate intellectuals or farmers or shopkeepers, either. Middle class people aren't free under this system. And ultimately we can make individual choices; we can resist capitalism, or not.

What I have learned to hate are the illusions and the opportunism that go along with middle class privilege. These are what continuously persuade the worker elite to join the other middle classes in embracing capitalism. They also motivate the class to manipulate, dominate, and strangle the freedom struggles of other workers for its own benefit.

The main force for revolution will come from within the working class. I believe that today, more than ever. But it will not come from the privileged worker elite. That's a deadly lie that has helped destroy the hopes of generations of radical activists and, more important, the hopes of generations of oppressed people.

Bromma

WORKING CLASS?

REVOLUTIONARIES OFTEN SAY THAT THE WORKING CLASS HOLDS the key to overthrowing capitalism. But "working class" is a very broad category—so broad that it can be used to justify a whole range of political agendas.

"Working class" is a useful popular expression, reflecting a diffuse social reality. We know that workers are the people who usually do the more unpleasant work of society. We know that workers are different from administrators or professionals or business owners or farmers or bankers. We know that working class people are generally afforded less prestige than other groups in society. When I was young, a lot of the Movement believed that factory workers, especially, were a core population around which broader working class practices, communities, values, and traditions revolved.

But if we try to examine the concept of the working class (or "working people") scientifically, it becomes elusive. Is the working class defined as wage earners? That leaves out housewives, most rural women, and slaves. Is the working class defined by manual labor? That leaves out tens of millions of poorly paid office and service workers. If your husband is working class, does that automatically make you working class? Is it true, as is endlessly repeated on the Left, that all the different kinds of workers all over the world are fundamentally "in the same boat"?

The phrase "working class" has a persistent descriptive power; it speaks to real differences in culture and caste. But over hundreds of years, it has come to span a hugely diverse range of social forces. In fact, "working class" doesn't really identify a single community of material interests under modern capitalism. It encompasses everyone from malnourished slaves in the colonial world to well-fed craft workers in the imperialist centers—people with very different lives, performing very different functions within capitalism. Certain parts of the working class—prison guards, for instance—have long existed to oppress other parts. Maybe we could make a special allowance for that in our theory somehow. But there's no way to finesse the fact that sizeable chunks of the working class have benefitted from—and therefore embraced—capitalism's program of privilege, national oppression, patriarchy, exploitation, and genocide. That's a reality too weighty to ignore.

One thing is clear: For the purpose of developing a revolutionary strategy, "working class" simply isn't specific enough.

THREE CLASSES

In fact, what is generally referred to as the working class isn't really a single class at all, but a family of three separate classes: the proletariat, the worker elite ("labor aristocracy"), and the lumpen working class ("lumpen-proletariat").[1] Although all three interact extensively, and share a lot of geographical and social terrain, each has its own specific class interests and politics.

The proletariat is made up of the slave, semi-slave, and heavily exploited workers who generate almost all of capitalism's profits. It is the "lower and deeper" part of the working class—and the overwhelming majority.

Since it lacks property ownership, social capital, and institutional privilege, the proletariat survives by working for other classes. The proletariat includes not only heavily exploited manufacturing workers but also huge populations of domestic, service, clerical, and agricultural workers. Mil-

4

lions of proletarians get no wages at all. Among these are a multitude of slaves, "peasant" women, and housewives. Millions of proletarians work outside the formal economy, or are unemployed, or are in prison. Hunger, deep poverty, and economic insecurity are completely normal conditions for the proletariat under capitalism. Child labor is widespread. The capitalist labor market pushes the proletariat's standard of living toward, or at times below, bare subsistence.

The lumpen is a parasitic class made up of people who live outside the web of "legal," above-ground production and distribution. It makes up a significant minority of the working class. The lumpen includes those who have been pushed or pulled out of the proletariat to become thieves, thugs, swindlers, gangsters, and warlords. It also includes working class people recruited into the repressive apparatus of the state—police, informants, prison guards, career soldiers, mercenaries, etc. The lumpen prey on all classes, but especially on the proletariat. In fact, from the viewpoint of the proletariat, the lumpen is basically a criminal class.[2]

The worker elite is the main subject of these notes. This is not, as some would maintain, a thin layer of trade union bureaucrats and craft workers. Rather, the worker elite is a mass class, comprising hundreds of millions of middle class workers around the world whose institutionalized privileges set them decisively apart from the proletariat. In short, entitled middle class workers. Although the absolute population of the worker elite world-wide is quite large, it makes up only a small fraction of the international working class.

The worker elite is part of a band of classes that exists "in the middle" between the proletariat and the bourgeoisie. The worker elite's middle class status comes into being when a particular subset of working class jobs—skilled or unskilled (see insert on next page)—is linked to institutionalized social bribery. This happens through a historical process of economic change, struggle, and negotiation with capital. The worker elite has its own unique class characteristics that distinguish it from other middle classes. But it

5

shares their position of privilege relative to the proletariat.

It's crucial to recognize the distinctions among the three classes that make up the "working class." They are embodied in sharp real-life contradictions: between slaves and overseers, between sweatshop seamstresses and six-figure crane operators, between immigrant farm workers and border cops, between day laborers and suburban homeown-

ONLY SKILLED LABOR?

Nineteenth century Marxists observed that working class privilege (in their time) was concentrated among the skilled craft workers, because these workers had economic leverage in the labor market and controlled the early craft-oriented unions. Soon enough revolutionaries began to realize that the profits of colonialism were being spread around to much broader sections of the imperial countries' working classes, while at the same time craft workers' leverage was actually declining. In 1858, Engels wrote to Marx, with some literary license, that "the British working class is actually becoming more and more bourgeois, so that this most bourgeois of all nations is apparently aiming ultimately at the possession of a bourgeois aristocracy and a bourgeois proletariat as well as a bourgeoisie. Of course, this is to a certain extent justifiable for a nation which is exploiting the whole world." ("To Marx," October 7, 1858)

By 1919, the First Congress of the Communist International, influenced by Lenin's new analysis of imperialism, put things this way: "At the expense of the plundered colonial peoples, capital corrupted its wage slaves, created a community of interest between the exploited and the exploiters as against the oppressed colonies—the yellow, black and red colonial people—and chained the European and American working class to the imperialist 'fatherland.'"

As we will see, worker elites have continued to expand and evolve, socially and geographically. Skilled work is no longer a pre-requisite for worker elite status. Neither is citizenship in a wealthy country.

ers, between health care aides and middle class pensioners, between machinists and drug dealers.

Downplaying these class contradictions is a recipe for political defeat. In fact, confusing or conflating the three classes is a common excuse for opportunism. Reformists and adventurists typically "substitute" the worker elite or the lumpen for the proletariat in justifying their political outlook.

Perhaps the most prominent example of this opportunist substitution is the deep-seated reformism that dominates the European and Euro-American Left today, including its "working class" sectors. This reformism has a solid material basis: the metropolitan Left is, with few exceptions, firmly rooted in the worker elite, and dedicated to promoting *its* class agenda—not the proletariat's. Its rhetoric about "working class struggle" and "working class unity" is a smokescreen, obscuring the Left's actual intention: to harness the proletariat in the interests of the labor elite and other privileged classes.

Maintaining clarity about the distinctions among the proletariat, the lumpen, and the worker elite, on the other hand, can help anchor our revolutionary politics in class reality.

These notes proceed from the proposition that revolutionary politics reflects the needs of the proletariat—not a loosely delineated "working class." In fact, for the proletariat to advance, it has to break decisively from the class politics of the worker elite and the lumpen.

What follows is an attempt to advance our analysis of the worker elite.[3] It is preliminary, partial, and (to be realistic) almost certainly incorrect in some ways. This important subject will require a lot more investigation and ideological struggle before it can fully inform modern revolutionary strategy. In the meantime, studying the worker elite as an independent class is a point of departure that can help illuminate important issues faced by radicals today, including the nature of trade unions and how to approach reform struggles.

FUNCTIONS OF THE WORKER ELITE

The worker elite has three main functions within modern imperialism.

1. First of all, it serves as an active buffer between the ruling class and the proletariat. This function has several aspects:

> A. The worker elite absorbs and co-opts proletarian struggle. When proletarian insurgency grows, the bourgeoisie responds with a mix of repression and social bribery to combat it. Systematic privilege may be extended to a section of the proletariat, offering tailored reforms and a preferential social contract in order to obtain that section's loyalty and divide it permanently from its rebellious counterparts.
>
> Emblematic of this process is Franklin Roosevelt's "New Deal," which effectively transformed millions of rebellious proletarian immigrants in the US into a loyal "white" worker elite. This corrupt arrangement seriously undermined proletarian solidarity and political struggle for generations, while simultaneously laying the foundation for the global projection of US imperial power.

Franklin Delano Roosevelt

B. The worker elite provides mass acquiescence and mass support for anti-proletarian politics, including settler colonialism, imperialist war, male domination, and genocide. The worker elite, because of its privileges, sees its fortune as tied to the fortune of the ruling class and therefore normally tries to help it succeed.

Again the New Deal provides a blueprint. In the 1930s, Roosevelt encouraged "white" US workers to join unions as part of an extensive national social contract. Yet at the exact same time, Puerto Rican trade unionists were being gunned down in the streets. Roosevelt was counting on "his" worker elite to accept this imperialist dichotomy—and for the most part, they have.[4] The ruling class relies on this specific kind of mass passivity and complicity to gain freedom of action in repressing the proletariat.

The worker elite's alliance with the ruling class is also expressed in more active forms in the arena of mass politics: elections, demonstrations, etc. The worker elite is a crucial element of many bourgeois parties. On an even more practical level, it's a routine practice and point of "honor" for children of the worker elite to fight and die in support of ruling class wars of aggression. The worker elite sometimes participates in direct repression of proletarian populations and anti-capitalist struggles. The labor elite is heavily represented in nativist and white supremacist groups in the US.

C. The worker elite influences and tries to dominate the proletariat politically and ideologically, asserting control over its struggles and organizations and constricting the limits of its dissent. For instance, the worker elite pushes itself forward as the "natural" leader of trade unions and other labor organizations, even those initiated and populated by proletarians. It lays claim to representing all working class interests in every arena of public discourse, including within the main capitalist political parties. The ruling class backs up this claim with ideological, political, and financial support.

D. The worker elite serves as an object of longing for the proletariat. It embodies living proof that some working class people can achieve privileged middle class lives. For many proletarians, the question then becomes not "how can we make revolution?" but "how can I become part of the worker elite?"

The worker elite's leadership actively encourages this wishful thinking. For example, the AFL-CIO (in many ways the world headquarters of the worker elite) has launched numerous initiatives in the US to organize immigrant workers from Latin America. In virtually every case, immigrants are encouraged to embrace "the American Dream" of privileged life in the metropolis as their only legitimate goal. Of course, most proletarian immigrants from Latin America never reach the promised "Dream." In reality, this is an invitation for workers to cut their ties with the labor movements in Latin America, movements which are often substantially more anti-capitalist and proletarian than those in the US. This approach also helps to divide Latin American workers from New Afrikan proletarians, who are, with limited exceptions, permanently and institutionally excluded from the "American Dream." The AFL-CIO approach is an attempt to increase its dues rolls and its leverage with the ruling class, while simultaneously grooming Latin American immigrants to function as a disciplined workforce for North American capitalism.

2. The second major function of the worker elite is as a class of mass consumption. Capitalism demands a growing spiral of investment, production, distribution, and sales. In our era, the capitalist economy will collapse unless mass populations purchase a constantly increasing volume of consumer products and services. Worker elite consumerism is an

economic imperative that dovetails with the other, political, functions of the class.

In his 1938 State of the Union address, in which he proudly proposed a minimum wage law, Roosevelt made the argument that "millions of industrial workers receive pay so low that they have little buying power," and were therefore "unable to buy their share of manufactured goods." He emphasized that this was a drag on the capitalist economy.[5]

The "social contract" between the worker elite and the ruling class is partly, in other words, a decision about which workers get to be middle class consumers.

In terms of consumerism, the upper end of the worker elite can even overlap other middle classes, including administrators, small business people, and professionals. Members of the worker elite sometimes mingle with other middle classes. These classes may live in the same neighborhoods, their kids may go to the same schools, etc. Children of the most privileged worker elite sometimes move into or marry into other middle classes.

3. The third major function of the worker elite is to supply labor to capitalist enterprises. Worker elites have potent privileges, but that doesn't give them a free pass. Most of the worker elite has to work to pay its bills. This function is a source of contradictions within the class.

A PARASITIC CLASS

Striving for middle class life is easy to understand on a human level. Everyone wants a better standard of living, for themselves and their children. Nevertheless, it is an unavoidable fact that the worker elite is an intrinsically parasitic class. The treasured privileges of the worker elite are funded by the ongoing capitalist exploitation of the proletariat; by the oppression of nations and women; by war, genocide, and rape of the natural environment. The rul-

ing class diverts a portion of the wealth that it derives from these sources to cultivating and maintaining worker elites, which in turn are persuaded to abandon and attack the proletariat and other enemies of capital. Unlike the proletariat, the character of the worker elite is not fundamentally determined by its labor. Rather, its class nature is fundamentally determined by its privileges. Its prized middle class status comes from a preferential social contract, approved and paid for by the bourgeoisie.

That middle class status doesn't come about because of greater skill, either. Within modern imperialism, technical education and skills are themselves privileges. Access to these privileges is controlled almost entirely by the bourgeoisie. So although most highly skilled workers are members of the worker elite, most members of the worker elite are no longer highly skilled workers.

In fact, worker elites often perform the same jobs performed by proletarians, under completely different conditions. For instance, middle class construction workers in the US have millions of proletarian counterparts (inside and outside the US) who live in desperate poverty and perform the same sorts of construction labor for a fraction of the pay.

The dramatic social disparity between them is the result of social bribery. Construction workers of the worker elite don't work harder than proletarians. Nor is their struggle against the employers more militant. In fact, the opposite is true: the worker elite has consistently helped to defeat or undercut the struggles of proletarian construction workers, choosing instead to defend its own privileges and its special arrangements with the ruling class. This choice isn't an expression of "false consciousness," as some radicals wishfully think. It's actual class consciousness, reflecting the worker elite's preferential status within imperialism.

Some people are confused by the fact that the worker elite is mostly made up of wage workers, who often perform unpleasant jobs. Plus, their work obviously contributes something to the the profitability of capitalist businesses,

keep geostrategic control over the places (like Bangladesh) where most of their profit originates. These ships, assembled in a complex and capital-intensive process, contain within them the accumulated labor of thousands of proletarians. For instance, the coke used in making the steel plate may have started out as coal from a mine in Africa where workers are paid pennies per hour. Electronic components may come from sweatshops in Asia. Each ship embodies thousands of hours of "hidden" unpaid work as well, at every stage of production. All this embedded labor, encapsulated in "lesser" commodities, is assembled by shipyard workers into gigantic, obscene, and unproductive weapons. In twenty five years they will have either sunk in battle or become obsolete hulks.

The ships are purchased by the US government. And that government is under virtual control of the financial trusts. So the capitalists are, in essence, selling this fabulously expensive merchandise to their own captive state. This is as much a scam as it is a production process.

Typically a fixed contract price will be set for warships, and any "unexpected costs" will simply be tacked on to what the government pays. Shipyards and their contractors routinely pad their expenses and payroll records, inventing

Secretary of Defense Leon E. Panetta speaks to the crew and workers from General Dynamics Electric Boat in front of the submarine USS Mississippi in Groton, Ct. on November 17, 2011.

extra costs to increase their earnings. Navy contracts are always lucrative, always highly coveted, and always doled out through a nakedly corrupt process that is almost never decided on the basis of labor price.

There's no drive to enforce starvation wages going on here. In fact, in this part of monopoly capital's food chain, providing the workers with middle class pay isn't that big a deal. On the contrary there are very good reasons for capitalists to do so.

For one thing, you can usually get away with billing the government multiple times for each worker. Why sweat the small stuff? Also, social peace is especially valuable in war-related industries (which happen to make up a large proportion of US industry today). For security reasons, the shipyard needs to be located inside the "homeland" and staffed by people supportive of its aims. These warships definitely aren't going to be outsourced to China. Once they are launched, the new ships will be crewed by the sons and daughters of people just like the shipyard workers, so there's no point in infuriating their parents. As a bonus, middle class shipyard workers will have enough money to buy more houses, cars, and consumer products. That can't hurt local businesses.

Of course the employers don't want to pay as high a wage as the shipyard workers ask. That would be excessive, and their shareholders would get mad. So there will be some friction with the labor force. But something can usually be worked out. Luckily for both sides, shipyard workers also get quite a few benefits directly from the state: unemployment insurance, social security, public education, etc. The most powerful capitalists have long agreed to this social arrangement to help maintain a loyal population in the US, one that will collaborate in the exploitation of proletarians— like those in Bangladesh. Someday that social contract may disappear, but that day is not here yet.

Shipyard workers hate paying taxes. But then again, a large proportion of those taxes go to military spending— which is exactly what keeps shipyard workers employed.

And so it is only logical that shipyard unions are constantly sending their officers (who may even be "leftists") to lobby in Congress for the construction of more warships.

Anyone who thinks shipyard work is fun or easy is in for a rude surprise if they actually try it. Especially if they are a woman or person of color. Nevertheless, US shipyard jobs are a clear example of parasitism in action. A group of privileged middle class workers makes their living by creating weapons of oppression, and begs the ruling class for more of the same. US shipyard workers, it turns out, aren't really that much like the garment workers in Bangladesh.

The parasitic dynamic extends far beyond the ranks of defense workers, of course. The US ruling class makes widespread use of social bribery to help it carry out a range of imperialist projects against the proletariat and oppressed nations, inside and outside North America. Other imperialist ruling classes do the same.

Historically, many worker elites arose first in the form of loyal populations in the imperial centers who benefited from settler colonialism and imperial aggression. Examples include the mass of English workers who supported the colonization of Ireland; the "white" workers who participated in Native genocide, slavery, colonialism, and racial segregation; the loyal ranks of Russian workers who championed Soviet social imperialism. This "classic" parasitic paradigm persists today. However, the worker elite has evolved, taking on new roles in support of consumerism, modern neocolonialism, and the latest wave of globalization.

There is another crucial sense in which the worker elite is parasitic: politically. Its rise feeds off the struggles of the proletariat. The harder proletarians fight to improve their conditions, the more the worker elite may be valued by the bourgeoisie. The more reforms the proletariat demands, the more opportunity there is for the worker elite to appropriate those reforms and turn them into privileges. Ripping off the proletarians' struggle, the worker elite succeeds at their expense.

A MALE CLASS

At the cultural, political, and demographic heart of the worker elite are male workers who do blue collar manual labor—teamsters, construction "hard hats," firefighters, machinists, well-paid manufacturing workers, etc.

The ideological outlook of the worker elite is macho. Although worker elite jobs are almost always less demanding than proletarian labor, they are nevertheless characteristically surrounded by a mythology of blue collar male toughness.

Historically, part of the ethos of the class has been the idea of a "family wage," according to which the "man of the family" is able to "provide for" everybody. The option of having a "stay-at-home wife" (whether exercised or not) is a key privilege of the worker elite, and continues to be an expectation in worker elites around the world, old and new. This privilege has a multiplier effect on household economic viability and standard of living.

The worker elite's maleness stands in direct contrast to the proletariat, which centers on women and their labor.[6] In fact the relationship between the worker elite and the proletariat echoes gender relations within the patriarchal nuclear family. Like the wife, the proletariat performs the

AFL and CIO leaders meet for "peace talks" in 1937.

hardest labor and endures the worst drudgery, often without pay. Like the husband, the worker elite carries out more prestigious, better-paid work, and attempts to dominate and control the proletariat. This analogy is rough, but not fanciful. In fact, in many households, proletarian women live side by side with men of the worker elite.

In recent decades, significant numbers of women have entered the worker elites of the imperialist metropolis, especially in the healthcare and public employment sectors. This development was given a push by working class women's struggle for equality. At the same time, it was adopted by the bourgeoisie as part of a pattern of neocolonial promotion of middle class women within multicultural capitalism. Who better to corral and control proletarian women today than other women?

However, the changes in the gender composition of the class are limited. Women continue to be excluded from many emblematic worker elite jobs, and patterns of male preference have carried over into the newer worker elites around the world, including those of rising imperialist countries. "Male" jobs continue to set the pattern for the allocation of privilege to the worker elite.

PROLETARIAT OR WORKER ELITE?

The dividing line between the proletariat and the worker elite is determined by several factors, which must be considered as a totality.

A privileged standard of living is a basic characteristic of worker elites. Standard of living is, of course, much more than wages and consumer spending; it also includes preferential social benefits—health insurance, pensions, vacation time, sick leave, unemployment insurance, etc. Economic privilege also may take the form of better education, home ownership, or greater access to infrastructure and services (transportation, the internet, indoor plumbing, etc.). Some privileges are negative—for instance, a relative absence of pollution or crime. Office work is less dirty and dangerous than most manual labor, which factors into some systems of worker privilege.

As mentioned above, the ability of a male worker to afford a stay-at-home housewife is a key privilege. In fact, a worker's ability to "provide for" a spouse and family on a single wage is an important economic data point in defining worker elites. Similarly, an exemption from child labor—something which is entirely "normal" in the proletariat—is a characteristic of worker elite households.

Inequality of income is a wedge that facilitates the creation of a worker elite. But the worker elite isn't just a bunch of better-paid workers. Beyond an improved standard of living, privilege is also modulated by workers' relationships to the political system, which enforces clear distinctions between the proletariat and the worker elite. Are worker protests encouraged, tolerated or repressed? Is there some form of government representation in place for workers? Are workers' unions recognized by the state? How are workers treated by the legal system? What are the patterns of incarceration?

Worker elites are typically positioned along already-existing fault lines in society, and often embody pre-existing patterns of social struggle. We have indicated that the worker elite and the proletariat are characteristically divided by gender. Worker elites are also organized along racial, national, religious, and industrial lines. For instance, the color line, an enduring mainstay of US settler capitalism, was central to the expansion of the worker elite during the New Deal. Masses of European immigrant workers who had previously been considered non-"white" were welcomed into "white" society as part of their elevation out of the proletariat.

The global rise of the worker elite was, and still is, intimately associated with colonialism. On the other hand, the contradiction between the worker elite and the proletariat isn't just a question of rich country workers versus poor country workers. Poor countries have worker elites, and rich countries have populations of proletarians.

This is critical to understand. Pretending that there are no worker elites in the Third World is a recipe for opportunism. At the same time, lumping together all the workers in the US or other wealthy countries as a "labor aristocracy" trivializes the struggles of the millions of proletarians, mostly from oppressed nationalities, who live and work there. (It also ignores the existence and separate class interests of the lumpen.)

An important characteristic that sets the worker elite apart is how systemic and durable its privileges are. Considering that class struggle ebbs and flows, and that capitalist labor markets are volatile, it's normal for some economic inequality to arise among proletarians. To cause something as consequential as a class distinction, privileges need to be significant and embedded into the fabric of society. In addition, middle class status must become hereditary. Otherwise, it's impossible for a separate class consciousness and culture to develop. Education and other forms of social grooming play a key role in passing on middle class status to the next generation.

We can only identify worker elites holistically. Economic advantages are certainly basic in demarcating the class, but historical and social factors are decisive. Above all else, a worker elite is defined by its preferential social contract with the bourgeoisie. This constitutes a specific structure of privileges, and a reciprocal benefit to the ruling class. A preferential social contract doesn't have to be a formal agreement or grand ruling class program like the New Deal. It can be as simple as a strategic commitment on the part of the bourgeoisie to create a new privileged worker/consumer class, in certain key industries, in exchange for patriotic loyalty and social peace. (This happened in Japan, and seems to be happening now in China, Brazil, and other industrializing countries.) Over time, systematic privilege becomes a stable "entitlement," providing the material basis for a separate middle class. This is a process we can readily study.

Despite what radical intellectuals often think, workers know quite a bit about where they are situated within class society. Thus it's typical for members of the worker elite to identify themselves as middle class. Of course, some workers may adopt that term merely as an aspiration. But for the most part, workers decide that they are middle class on a very practical basis: their distinct, all-around preferential status as wage earners, consumers, and "citizens." These workers believe themselves to be separate in essential ways from the proletariat. We should take this perception seriously.

INCOME INEQUALITY

To analyze privilege in the working class, we must first come to grips with the current pattern of world economic inequality. On one level this means looking at a bunch of boring statistics. On another level it means seeing the real working class come alive before our eyes.

A lot of our analysis depends on what numbers we look at. Neither "average" wages nor "median" wages give us a clear view of how income is actually distributed inside the working class. These metrics actually obscure some of the most important vectors of inequality. Simply converting wages paid in one country's currency into another country's is also grossly misleading, since the cost of living varies radically from country to country (and even within countries).

In recent decades, bourgeois economists have developed improved statistical tools to compare global income. These so-called "purchasing power parity" (PPP) calculations crunch large amounts of data: wage rates, currency fluctuations, taxes, cost of living, etc. They factor in the price of over 1,000 goods and services in each country, usually sampled from several different regions. PPP income is calculated in equivalent US dollars (usually using 2005 or 2006 as a baseline). Combining cost of living, income, taxes, and currency conversion into a single figure this way allows economists to begin to level the statistical playing field.

While far from perfect, PPP calculations make it possible to estimate and compare real income and spending power in different parts of the world on a common scale. A worker making PPP $10,000 in Indonesia or Zimbabwe will have roughly the same standard of living as a worker making PPP $10,000 in Canada or France.[7]

Capitalists developed these statistics for their own purposes, including global economic strategy and marketing. It turns out they are also useful for revolutionaries studying the changing international working class. They allow us to examine income inequality in a relatively straightforward and detailed manner, revealing formerly obscure patterns of class oppression and privilege.

As a starting point for investigating these patterns, a primitive "ladder" of PPP normalized income has been assembled below. This ladder is based on approximate net personal income. In most cases this income is given directly in PPP wages. In other cases (for instance, in the case of children) the figure provided is a calculation, using PPP household income and dividing it by the number of household members. Where US (non-PPP) wages are cited, 20% has been deducted for taxes to make them roughly comparable to PPP wages, which already have taxes and other mandatory fees subtracted.

These are *individual, annual* amounts:

$0   Slaves. Estimates of the number of
            slaves in the world vary widely, rang-
            ing from 4 million to tens of millions.[8]
            Almost all slaves are workers, per-
            forming agricultural, manufacturing,
            domestic, and sex labor. There are
            also uncounted millions of virtual
            slave women, laboring without pay in
            households and on small farms. A good
            deal of prison labor is unpaid or paid a
            token amount.

PPP $456 or less	Approximately 1.3 billion people; "absolute poverty."[9]
PPP $730 or less	($2,920 for a family of four.) 2.44 billion people.[10] Many workers in the informal sector fall into this category—garbage pickers, battery recyclers, unlicensed child care workers, street corner peddlers, etc. 2.8 million children inside the US fall into this income category; that number is rising.[11]
PPP $1,100	Garment workers, Bangladesh, whose PPP yearly wage *fell* slightly between 2001 and 2011.[12]
PPP $1,900	Minimum wage, rural China. (Highest—urban—minimum wage: $2,850.)[13]
PPP $2,750 or less	Individuals in 20 million US households. This group is growing rapidly.[14]
PPP $3,650 or less	80% of the world's people.[15] This is an important metric, discussed further below.
PPP $4,500	Average US welfare (AFDC) payment, 2006.[16]
PPP $4,800	Average private sector wage, China.[17] (Public sector wages are usually higher.)
PPP $5,080	Full time Chilean domestic workers.[18]
PPP $5,755	US official poverty level, 2012. (This is based on a figure of $23,021 for a family of four.) Nearly 50 million people in the US are at or below this level.[19]
PPP $8,980	South Korean (full time) minimum wage, 2010.[20]
PPP $10,600	Express delivery drivers, China.[21]
PPP $12,400	English language call center workers, India.[22]
PPP $14,000	Auto assembly workers, China, 2010.[23]

PPP $15,000	Migrant farm workers, US.[24]
PPP $15,900	High rise window washers, China.[25]
PPP $18,500	Meatpacking workers, US, 2006.[26]
PPP $30,700	US manufacturing workers, average, 2012.[27]
PPP $43,000	Auto assembly workers, Korea.[28]
PPP $44,800	X-ray technicians, US.[29]
PPP $50,000	Factory maintenance technicians, Brazil.[30]
PPP $58,000 to $70,000	Auto assembly workers, US, Germany, Japan.[31]
PPP $100,000	Full time dockworkers, US.[32]

Radical income inequality in the working class is an inescapable fact.

Everybody knows that there is inequality between workers in wealthy countries and in poor countries. This often carries across all categories of work. For instance, US workers take in three and a half to four times the PPP income of their counterparts in Thailand, something that holds true whether we look at auto assembly or garment manufacture.[33]

However there have been important changes in the geography of "country vs. country" inequality over the last several decades. For instance, Japan, Singapore, Hong Kong, Macau, Taiwan, South Korea, Israel, and areas of Eastern Europe and the Persian Gulf have become part of the developed "global north." Moreover, emerging imperialist powers such as China and Brazil are moving rapidly to exploit low-wage workers in other countries. For instance, Chinese capitalists have invested billions of dollars in Zambia and employ tens of thousands of workers there. These workers are sometimes heavily exploited and abused, and may receive much lower wages than Chinese workers in the same industries. (see insert next two pages)

MAMBA COLLUM MINE

Chinese investment has reportedly generated some 50,000 jobs in Zambia, with trade between the two countries reaching $3.5 billion in 2011.

In 2012, the Zambian government passed a law mandating a substantial raise in the legal minimum wage (at that time, it was PPP $924 a year for most workers. See ILO *Global Wage Report*, 2010/11). But Chinese mine owners flatly refused to pay the new minimum:

> *Workers are demanding the immediate imposi-*
> *tion of the new minimum wage and a dispute*
> *over its delay saw mineworkers kill a Chinese su-*
> *pervisor and seriously injure two other Chinese*
> *nationals on August 4 at the Mamba Collum*
> *Coal Mine, about 300 km south of Lusaka.*
> *According to local media reports, one miner*
> *has been charged with murder and 11 others*
> *have been charged with rioting and theft, after*
> *mineworkers also stole computers and office*
> *furniture during the protests.*
>
> *"The new minimum wage is not supposed to*
> *affect unionized employees because they are*
> *all bound by the rules of collective bargaining,*

and are supposed to get far above the minimum wage. But what is sad is that some of our employers pay even far below the stipulated minimum wage," president of the Mineworkers Union, Chishimba Nkole, told IRIN.

A miner at Mamba Collum Coal Mine, who declined to be named, told IRIN he receives a monthly "take home" pay of $80.

"We were very excited when the government announced the new minimum wage. But now, these Chinese [employers] are refusing to increase our salaries and are instead telling us that they will have to fire over half of the workers to pay the minimum wage," the coal miner said....

Two Chinese supervisors were charged with attempted murder after 13 Zambian miners were shot during a wage dispute two years ago at the same Mamba Collum Coal Mine. The charges were later dropped.[34]

The Mamba Collum Mine has since been closed by the Zambian government, citing "safety concerns."[35]

Another dramatic form of inequality exists between workers in different industries. Auto assembly workers make two to three times what textile workers earn no matter where we look in the world.[36] We should not be surprised that auto assembly workers are overwhelmingly men, while textile workers are mostly women.

This raises a point that is often underappreciated by radicals: income inequality inside countries is usually just as glaring as income inequality between countries. In the US, the bottom 20% of households took in 3.2% of total income in 2011.[37] In 2012, the bottom 25% of China's households accounted for 3.9% of total income, a roughly similar result.[36] Income differentials of 20 times or more within a single country's working class are not uncommon. These kinds of differential can be far bigger than the average differential between workers in rich and poor countries. Slavery and "absolute poverty" co-exist with strata of middle class workers, even in countries that are, on average, extremely poor.

Meanwhile, wages at the top of the working class income ladder are starting to converge across national lines. This is especially true between the newly-industrializing countries and the older imperialist centers. The phenomenon of middle class workers is truly transnational today.

QUANTITY INTO QUALITY: MIDDLE CLASS WORKERS

The great majority of workers around the globe are extremely poor by any standard. This leads us to an obvious question: Is there a particular rung on the income ladder where elevated income and standard of living begin to function as privilege? Is there an identifiable point at which quantity turns into quality, where class differentiation into a worker elite begins; where workers with higher incomes start to become detached, objectively and subjectively, from the proletariat?

For many years, it has been customary to view the "labor aristocracy" as a "First World" phenomenon, something barely worth considering in the rest of the world. This leads to somewhat simplistic theories that contrast workers in "rich countries" to those in "poor countries." The best analysis based on this data can easily prove (again) something revolutionaries should certainly already know by now: that there is a dramatic difference between the average income of Third World workers and their counterparts in the US and Europe.[38] But this approach fails to identify worker elites in other, less stereotypical situations—for instance, inside multinational settler states, within the Third World itself, or within particular transnational industries.

If worker elites in rich countries get three or four times the income of workers in poor countries, how should we think about similar income discrepancies that exist inside the poor countries? Do those also signal the existence of a worker elite? Is there an absolute income cutoff of some kind for the worker elite? Or is privilege mainly relative? (And if so, is it relative to other workers domestically, internationally or both?)

In struggling to define the "labor aristocracy," traditional Marxist economists often try to figure out a specific pay level at which workers are no longer technically "exploited"—that is, a level where their wages are so high that their labor generates no actual profit to the world capitalist system. They then attempt to use this pay level to identify worker elites and differentiate them from "non-aristocratic" workers.

Yet even on a strictly economic level, this is an extremely problematic calculation. For one thing, it requires factoring into account massive amounts of unpaid labor, which is a "hidden" component of all the wages actually paid under capitalism. (How could exploited factory workers survive and generate profit without all the unpaid work carried out by the rest of the proletariat?) Actually, the sector of workers who perform informal and unwaged labor in a given country is frequently larger than the waged sector, once we take all women's labor into account. This quickly leads into a statistical quagmire. The "exploitation line" becomes an indirect calculation, sometimes depending less on rigorous science than on methodology and preconception.

Attempts to define this kind of "exploitation line" often fall back on archaic metrics. For instance, they typically rely on statistics for average national male manufacturing wages, which are the easiest figures to obtain and compare. (They also fit most neatly into conventional academic Marxist economic models.) We have already seen, however, that "average wage" figures can conceal as much as they reveal, by evening out enormous differences in standard of living within each country. And of course male manufacturing wage data simply excludes too much of the working class to adequately characterize working class reality.

These notes will attempt to analyze worker privilege from another angle. Using PPP income data now available, they will try to identify at what point on the global income ladder workers are—and also consider themselves to be—middle class. They will argue that the emergence of a stratum of middle class workers is central to the rise of the worker elite.

This alternate approach has its own complications. It's hard to define a middle class standard of living exactly. There are a lot of variables involved, including wages, taxes, family size, exchange rates, and local cost of living. Nevertheless, current PPP economic data does allow us to

approximately demarcate a global middle class, yielding a clearer and more fine-grained understanding of the distribution of economic privilege.

In recent decades, as PPP income data has become available, there have been several statistical models put forward by economists to define middle class income and middle class standard of living.[39] After years of debate, they have converged on the metric adopted by the World Bank, IMF, and other global capitalist agencies: more than PPP $10 a day per person ($3,650 a year), but below PPP $100 a day per person ($36,500 a year). As a reminder, these figures are for net income, after taxes and other mandatory charges are stripped out.

> *The lower bound is chosen with reference to the average poverty line in Portugal and Italy, the two advanced European countries with the strictest definition of poverty. The poverty line for a family of four in these countries is USD $14,533 (USD $9.95 per day per capita in 2005 purchasing power parity terms). The upper bound is chosen as twice the median income of Luxemburg, the richest advanced country. Defined in this way, the global middle class excludes those who are considered poor in the poorest advanced countries and those who are considered rich in the richest advanced country.[40]*

As we would expect, this definition encompasses most of the population of the rich countries, but includes only a few percent of the urban population of poorer countries like India or Cambodia. China falls somewhere in the middle. There, it includes some 12–15% of the Chinese population.[41]

It was mentioned in the income ladder above, but has to be highlighted once again: 80% of the world's people fall below this definition of middle class income. This gives us some clues to the potential size of the global worker elite. We know that hundreds of millions of "middle class" people in this (PPP $3,650–$36,500) income range aren't workers at all. They are professionals, shopkeepers, administrators, small farmers, businesspeople, intellectuals, etc. Therefore the percentage of workers, specifically, who have middle class income is much smaller than 20%. We can confidently estimate that fewer than 10% of all workers are middle class by this definition.

Even so, is it a capitalist marketing fantasy to say that a person making a net income of PPP $3,600 a year (or a four-person household making PPP $14,600 a year) is middle class? Probably not. Nancy Birdsall, in her study of households in Peru, Chile, and Mexico, found that people who reached this level of income were highly unlikely to fall back into deep poverty over time. She also found that "it was at or around $10 a day that respondents identified themselves as middle class rather than poorer."[43]

Where income reaches PPP $10 a day per family member, economists observe that household spending patterns change rapidly. Since they have met their most basic survival needs, and feel relatively secure from falling into deep poverty, households start buying certain kinds of durable goods—used cars, washing machines, refrigerators, etc. Cell phones are common. Workers just slightly higher on the income scale use increased discretionary income for things like new cars, higher education, better clothes, computers, more varied diet, home ownership, vacation travel, etc.

This is a global phenomenon, not something that happens only, or even primarily, in the global north. The World

Bank says that "Plane tickets ... are one of the most purchased items among Brazil's emergent middle class. Between July 2011 and July 2012 alone, 9.5 million Brazilians flew for the first time."[44] 550–600 million people in the developing world with incomes between PPP $10 and PPP $50 a day have the use of a family car (often a used vehicle).[45] Tata Motors is now targeting this consumer segment with plans to market a new automobile that will sell for just over PPP $2,000, with low monthly payment plans available.[46]

> *Survey evidence ... suggests China's new middle class is eager to become the world's leading consumers. A 2007 survey of 6,000 Chinese shoppers found that Chinese consumers spend 9.8 hours per week shopping, as compared to only 3.6 hours for the typical American (Chan and Tse, 2007). Additionally more than 40 per cent of Chinese survey respondents said shopping was a favourite leisure activity. It is such attitudes that have led global retailers to bet on the future of China's domestic market: in the 13 years since opening its first store in China, Wal-Mart has gone on to open an additional 257 retail units (Wal-Mart, 2009).[47]*

These are markers of a qualitative change in standard of living; they involve a level of consumption completely beyond the reach of the poor 90% of workers. A study of so-called "developing countries" found that 61% of the households there have PPP income below $13,500 a year. These so-called "deprived" households consume just 28% of all goods and services—less than half of what should be their population's proportional share of the national total. Households with incomes of PPP $13,500 to $22,500 consume roughly twice as much per household: 23.6% of the population at this income level accounts for 23% of the goods and services purchased. In the study's next higher bracket—PPP $22,500 to PPP $56,499—13% of households account for 32% of all spending. In other words, this group consumes more than five times as much per family as the "deprived" majority.[48]

Household income is the key metric to look at. A worker trying to support a family of four on PPP $4,000 a year certainly isn't middle class. Even if two household members earn that wage, the family as a whole will be well short of middle class status.

We have noted previously that among worker elites there is an expectation that a single income—usually that of the "man of the house"—should be able to keep a whole family out of poverty. Using this standard, a global middle class annual income probably starts somewhere between PPP $10,000 and $15,000. (Gross wages, we should remember, would be slightly higher.)

Privilege may be relative as well as absolute. For many of us living inside the bubble of the wealthiest economies, a Chinese auto assembly worker's income of PPP $14,000 doesn't sound high. It's not that much above the official US individual poverty line. But compared to a Chinese sweatshop worker making PPP $3,000 (or a Zambian worker in a Chinese-owned coal mine making even less) it constitutes a significant advantage. Not only can the autoworker buy more, but they can afford to support a middle class family on a single income. (Average family size in China is three.)

This is exactly the kind of economic division that capitalists in every part of the world recognize and manipulate; exactly the kind of economic division that makes worker elites possible.

There's no magic income figure delineating the boundary of the proletariat. The PPP $10–15,000 figure is a useful data point in the stratification of the working class, but that's all. It would be wrong to think that every worker with net income above $15,000 a year has left the proletariat. As we have discussed, non-economic factors are decisive in the definition of worker elites. And privilege may look different in different societies. Family size alone is a major variable from one place to another.

But it would also be wrong to think that the dramatic differentials in net income, standard of living, and consumer status we have been looking at are irrelevant to class being, class consciousness, and class behavior in modern imperialism.

Looking at normalized world income, it's irrefutable that a meaningful percentage of workers in the developing world—and a majority of workers in the wealthy countries—have a lot more to lose than their chains. Many millions of those workers are established at a qualitatively higher standard of living than the huge impoverished proletarian majority. Their principal economic concern isn't survival, but maintaining and enhancing their middle class status. These workers meet the minimum economic requirements for the worker elite.

Satyananda J. Gabriel writes, "The very process by which workers are changed into consumers, where personal identity becomes intertwined with the specific bundle of commodities possessed, where work is seen only as means to acquisition of such commodities (as it is within the neoclassical parables), is one in which consciousness of class is obliterated and exploitation normalized."[19] Agreed. But also, within the vacuum created by the obliteration of proletarian consciousness, a new worker elite class consciousness is easily forged.

OLD CLASS, NEW CLASS

It's easy to fall into old-fashioned thinking about the worker elite as being merely a subset of the division between the First World and the Third World. And it's understandable that radicals might think that way, since most of the profits that pay for worker elite privileges have come historically from colonial theft, extortion, and exploitation. Besides, the worker elite, even today, exists in concentrated form in the wealthiest Western countries. But this duality, which once provided a sort of rough and ready rule of thumb, doesn't fully illuminate either the national or international characteristics of the worker elite today.

For generations there has been a multitude of established worker elites in Asia, Africa, and Latin America. And now, within a new wave of globalization, modern imperialism is trending towards a broadly distributed and truly international worker elite. Finance capital is drastically reducing its dependency on social bribery in the US and Europe. Privilege, it appears, now gives more bang for the buck elsewhere. Emerging worker elites, including those in poor countries, are starting to provide the new consumer markets and political buffers that imperialism requires most for its survival.

The IMF, global capital's hatchet man, has long argued that a key benefit of "free trade" in the Third World is that "new jobs are created for unskilled workers, raising them into the middle class."[50] The ruling class actively promotes this trend, and chases after the new consumers it produces in the "developing world," just like Franklin Roosevelt's capitalist cronies once did inside the US. This transformative class dimension of globalization also permits and encourages the ruling class to abrogate many old, long-established domestic social contracts in the West, and replace them with new forms of international social bribery.

The geographic expansion of privilege is particularly obvious right now in Asia, because the bulk of world economic activity is relocating there. This is something widely accepted among economists.

By 2034, 25 years from now, the global economy may be USD *$200 trillion in* PPP *dollars. Such a world [would be] very different from the one we see today....*

The economic centre of gravity would shift to Asia, which accounts today for 34 per cent of global activity, but by 2034 could account for 57 per cent of global output. Three giant economies, China, India and Japan, would lead Asia's resurgence. But other large countries like Indonesia and Vietnam would also have significant economic mass. Even Thailand and Malaysia could have economies larger than France has today.

The rise of Asia would not be unprecedented. Indeed, it would bring Asia's economic share into line with its population share and restore the balance of global economic activity to that in the 18th and early 19th centuries, before the Industrial Revolution led to the great divergence of incomes across countries.[51]

It's been estimated that by 2030, Asia will have 66% of the world's middle class population and will account for 59% of middle class consumption.[52]

We may be tempted to dismiss bourgeois economists' celebration of the rising Asian middle class as wishful thinking, and some of it surely is. Given the fragility of the current world economy, the most optimistic projections of middle class expansion in Asia are probably unrealistic. But the trend is still clear. While wages are stagnant or falling in the Western metropolis, wages in Asia have doubled since 2000.[53] And large groups of Asian workers have become privileged.

Decades ago, Japan was a trailblazer in institutionalizing a large Asian worker elite. But today it is far from unique. Heavy capitalist investment in the South Korean shipbuilding and auto industries has been accompanied by the growth of a worker elite roughly modeled on those of the West and Japan. In 2011, the average compensation costs for manufacturing workers in South Korea was almost $19 (US) an hour, according to the Bureau of Labor Statistics. This despite the fact that millions of proletarians in South Korea live in dire poverty.

Recently the Chinese government announced a national crusade for better pay for its workers, part of a planned shift away from export industries and towards internal consumption as the main engine of its economy. "China's middle class today is already large in absolute terms—at 157 million people, only the United States has a larger middle class."[54] It's likely that there will soon be a Chinese worker elite that is larger and more important politically than any that exists in the Western countries.

Outside of Asia, other industrializing countries also have growing worker elites. Brazilian manufacturing workers are a pillar of the new capitalist order in Brazil.

> *There is no doubt Brazil is an emerging imperialist power. It dominates the Latin America economy, exports capital, is a major factor in markets around the world, is expanding its military capacity and intervenes politically to assert its growing influence, gaining on the decaying US Empire....*
>
> *Brazilian exports have tripled since 2003 on rising world demand for everything it produces. Brazil, once the world's largest emerging-market debtor, became a net foreign creditor for the first time in 2011 as international reserves swelled to a record $171.6 billion from $37.6 billion at the start of 2003. Brazil is the sole capital exporter in Latin America....*
>
> *Brazil has one of the highest disparity rates of poverty versus wealth in the world.... In the favelas... 52% of the populace is not connected to potable water distribution, 68% have no garbage collection and*

78% are not connected to sanitary sewage disposal or septic tanks.

Add to that 25% do not have electricity and 74% live in households where the head of the household has less than four years of schooling. These appalling conditions are the subtext for high rates of criminal activity, inequality and the frustrating inability of the poor to develop their human potential. For women this all goes double....

Add these conditions to the racial discrimination against the indigenous populace and against the descendents of the four million slaves brought to Brazil from Africa. Although slavery was abolished in Brazil over a hundred years ago, access to education, land, health care, rights to their land titles and employment are still problems for slave descendents. Racism is a big part of the Brazilian economic miracle....[55]

[Author: In fact, Brazilians considered "Black" earn about 58% of what "white" Brazilians earn.[56]*]*

The Central Única dos Trabalhadores (Unified Workers' Central, known by the acronym CUT), is the main union confederation in Brazil. The CUT was formed in 1983 based on the auto and metal workers unions organized in the manufacturing suburbs around Sao Paulo. It is the main base of the Workers' Party (PT).

It is from the CUT and the PT [that] Inácio Lula da Silva (Lula), a former metal workers union leader and leader of the CUT, rose from impoverished shoeshine boy to be an extremely popular prime minister and world figure. The workers that formed the CUT paid with their blood, sweat and tears to be a large component of the forces that overthrew the Brazilian military dictatorship.

> *Lula and the PT however lead a government of
> class conciliation designed to introduce just enough
> reforms to win the critical loyalty of the Brazilian
> working class for the imperialist project of the ruling
> class...*
>
> *It is the same process by which the trade unions in the
> USA and the British Labour Party for example won
> their roles in their national political systems as labor
> aristocrats or privileged workers.*[57]

The broadening geographical distribution of privilege is an important change. But as it evolves, modern imperialism is taking an even bigger step. It's gradually detaching itself from the model of privileged "home countries" altogether. Finance capital floats above national borders, exploiting an increasingly mobile proletariat. Seeking to optimize the use of privilege under these new conditions, capitalists sometimes bypass national bourgeoisies entirely. Multinational industries, corporations, and financial trusts now purchase loyalty and disburse privilege directly, "over the heads" of any specific country or any national ruling class.

Consider, for instance, the relatively new layer of non-technical English-speaking call center workers in India. The rise of the Indian call centers required a series of changes in the world economy: advanced global internet technology, diffusion of a cosmopolitan culture, weakening of Western social contracts, institutional support for transnational outsourcing and wage arbitrage, etc. To make their business model work, the call centers need unskilled workers who speak good English and who are willing to do repetitive, stressful

work. To attract these workers, the employers are willing to pay about twice what a high school teacher, accountant or MBA marketing professional earns, 20 to 30 times what an Indian construction worker makes. Most of the current call center workers are young and unmarried, and most of them have no special training or advanced degrees.

Although their work is unpleasant, forcing them to interact for hours on end with disgruntled and chauvinist overseas customers, the call center workers do lead middle class lives. They often get employee perks like free food, transportation, and special leisure activities provided by the employers.

It may be too soon to say if this group of workers will become fully established as a cohort of the Indian national worker elite. The workforce is still evolving. What's notable about their privilege, in any case, is that it depends not on the Indian domestic economy, or on India's imperial ambitions, but on the international marketplace for business services. The call center industry is controlled by multinational finance capital, not Indian national capitalists. This puts workers in a contradictory position.

> *Call-center employees gain their financial independence at the risk of an identity crisis. A BPO [call center] salary is contingent on the worker's ability to de-Indianize: to adopt a Western name and accent and, to some extent, attitude. Aping Western culture has long been fashionable; in the call-center classroom, it's company policy. Agents know that their jobs only exist because of the low value the world market ascribes to Indian labor. The more they embrace the logic of global capitalism, the more they must confront the notion that they are worth less.*[58]

It's routine for call center workers to migrate outside of India in the course of their careers, if only temporarily, to maintain or enhance their class position. "Companies such as Tata Consultancy Services, Genpact and Infosys are the

largest users of the US-American H-1B visa program and have collectively brought as many as 30,000 workers into the country in 2010."[59] Other call center workers travel outside India as trainers. The call center workers are part of a new transnational pattern of privilege, linked not just to a greater India, but to globalization and neo-liberalism.

Changes in the worker elite inside US borders give us another window into how neocolonialism is transforming worker privilege.

In response to the national liberation movements of the 1960s and 70s, the US ruling class permitted and even encouraged the rise of (relatively small) Black and Chicano/Mexicano worker elites. These are worker elites within internal colonies—something which right away sets them apart from the classic colonial paradigm.

First of all, it would be a mistake to conflate these oppressed nation worker elites with the worker elite of the oppressor nation (the US). They are tied to their own national societies and class structures, and therefore often play different political roles from the "white" worker elite. For instance, New Afrikan and Chicano/Mexicano worker elites in the US constantly struggle to open up more "good jobs" for people of color in the teeth of racist discrimination. This goes entirely against the default politics of the "white"

42

worker elite, which instinctively favors segregating and excluding oppressed nationality workers from better paying jobs and social opportunities.

But just as with the Indian call center workers, the privileges of Black and Chicano/Mexicano worker elites are enabled and funded not by their "own" national bourgeoisies but by multinational corporations and international finance capital. This fosters class loyalties outside the oppressed nations—to multinational corporate interests specifically and to global capitalism generally. The ruling class expects to get "two for one" from these worker elites: weakened proletarian militancy and diluted revolutionary nationalism.

Imperialism has simultaneously seized the opportunity to weaken the old settleristic US social contract. Among "white" workers, real wages are stagnant, unemployment is high, unions are dwindling, and social benefits and protective regulations are evaporating. White workers are still heavily privileged in relation to oppressed nationality workers overall. But a subset of Black and Latino workers have surpassed their white counterparts economically. Also, large numbers of iconic worker elite jobs have been relocated overseas or transformed into proletarian jobs, much to the vocal dismay of their former "white" occupants.

The message—sent and received—is that in this new globally integrated, multicultural capitalist system, being a "white" worker is no longer an automatic guarantee of top privilege. Still a big advantage, but one that can be withdrawn at any time.

This constitutes a dramatic change in the organization of social bribery in the US empire. For hundreds of years, the ruling class enforced rigid national segregation of elite jobs. This segregation, implemented through a violently enforced "color line," was a key defining feature of the worker elite in the US. But now the multinational bourgeoisie routinely supports the integration, offshoring, and downgrading of what used to be "white" worker elite jobs, pushing aside resentful "white" opposition as needed. The emergence of this new set of contradictions—the rise of new worker elites and the destruction of old settler social contracts—is an integral part of the evolution of neocolonialism.

None of these changes benefit the proletariat, at least not directly. Oppressed nationalities as a whole don't benefit either. Privilege is being reconfigured precisely so that the ruling class can enhance its dominance under the new conditions of modern capitalism. Colonialism has been reorganized, not eliminated.

The rise of neocolonial labor elites has in fact widened and solidified the divisions between colonial proletariats and their own national middle classes. As the bourgeoisie hoped, it has weakened labor insurgency and the struggle for national liberation. The rise of oppressed nationality worker elites proceeds hand in hand with the continued destruction of proletarian communities in the colonial world. Vicious national oppression, including genocide, continues without pause.

In the long run, there is a possibility that as worker privilege becomes more mobile and transnational, it may also become less stable. The old-line worker elites of the West have survived for more than a century and a half. Japanese and Korean worker elites have lasted for generations. But the longevity of the new Brazilian, New Afrikan,

and Mexicano/Chicano worker elites remains to be determined. (Some Indian call center jobs, we note, are already migrating to the Philippines.) Today, economic and political change occurs at an accelerated rate. If worker privileges come and go rapidly enough, they may lose their durable, hereditary character. This could weaken the worker elite as a class, and might eventually provide new political opportunities for the proletariat.

What's crucial to recognize is that privilege is gradually transcending its old boundaries. As the worker elite evolves within neocolonialism, some of its national loyalties will erode (like the capitalists' national loyalties already have). That trend will be uneven, and will probably affect the outlook of the class in unexpected ways. Worker elites of the future may be more loyal to specific corporations, pools of capital or global capitalist strategies than to their nations or countries of birth. To analyze the changing interests of the modern worker elite, whether inside or across national borders, we can only continue to follow the money trail of imperial privilege and the neocolonial social contracts by which it makes its way to the class.

CONTRADICTIONS WITH THE PROLETARIAT

The worker elite puts itself forward as the sole rightful representative of the working class as a whole. This is completely fraudulent, since the worker elite has no control at all over the lumpen, and "represents" the proletariat only as its overseer. As we would expect, the ruling class enthusiastically endorses the pretense of worker elite "leadership," anointing that class as its principal bargaining partner in the working class. The labor elite and the bourgeoisie work together to suppress and undermine independent proletarian leadership and initiative.

The worker elites' unions and its union bureaucrats advise the bourgeoisie about how to channel labor militancy and divvy up privilege. Politically, worker elites often work closely with the reformist wing of the ruling class. They lobby energetically for the principle that (certain) worthy workers deserve to be thrown a bone from the capitalist feast. The worker elite alliance with the bourgeoisie is characteristically embodied in a range of liberal and social-democratic parties, including decayed ex-socialist parties.

We have noted that the worker elite is parasitic on the proletariat, and that it sometimes plays a direct repressive role. However, this class relationship is far from simple. The

45

labor elite wants to grow, as long as their privileges don't get diluted. Besides, without the threat of proletarian rebellion, the worker elite loses some of its leverage with the ruling class. Why should the capitalists accommodate privileged workers if they are no longer needed as a buffer?

In fact, ironically, the current decline of worker elites in the old imperial metropolis results partly from the weakness of proletarian revolution, domestically and internationally. The New Deal and other Western social contracts accomplished everything the bourgoisie had dreamed of, and now it's time for the capitalists to move on to "new" New Deals elsewhere. The old-line worker elites did their job only too well, undermining their own future as they helped the bourgeoisie split, suppress, and corrupt the massive worldwide wave of proletarian struggles after WWII.

All worker elites face this deep contradiction: There needs to be a certain amount of proletarian struggle to justify their privileged existence, yet one of their basic class functions is precisely to control such struggle and prevent it from succeeding.

These contradictory material interests often cause the worker elite to view the proletariat with cold-blooded calculation. The proletariat needs to be kept in check, of course. But on the other hand, the proletariat's tenacious willingness to struggle and sacrifice might make them useful as "shock troops" for the worker elite. Proletarian combativeness can buffer the worker elite from the capitalists, just as the worker elites buffer the capitalists from the proletariat.

When the worker elite wishes to employ the proletariat for leverage, its "anti-establishment" aspect and rebellious rhetoric may come to the fore; the worker elite may even provide political or material assistance to proletarian struggles. At the same time, true to its fundamental class nature, the worker elite will work to control, manipulate, and eventually defeat such struggles.

One historical example of this contradictory dynamic is the US worker elite's response to the dramatic struggle unleashed by the National Farmworkers' Association and its successor, the United Farm Workers, in the 1960s and 70s. This history has relevance to present-day struggles of poor workers, such as the current "Fight for 15" and fast food worker campaigns, both of which are heavily funded and substantially directed by worker elite forces (including the leadership of the Service Employees International Union).

When the UFW emerged in the 1960s, it was a militant proletarian social movement that showed signs of radically transforming working class politics in the US. It was pivotal in the rise of a powerful Chicano movement, and incorporated a novel alliance between Mexican and Filipino field workers. Women were actively recruited as organizers by the union. Led by charismatic activists Cesar Chavez and Dolores Huerta, its original social base was mainly among "legal," documented workers. The UFW was widely regarded on the Left as a labor movement with tremendous revolutionary potential.

At first, most of the US worker elite reacted to the UFW as if it were an invading enemy. The Teamsters Union, at that time the largest union in the country, achieved everlasting infamy by signing sweetheart contracts with management to exclude the UFW, and by organizing goon squads to brutalize and kill UFW workers.

But other parts of the worker elite leadership cautiously welcomed the UFW, seeing not only an opportunity to enlarge the "mainstream" labor movement, but also a chance to re-invigorate and diversify their trade union coalition, strengthen their hand in bargaining with the ruling class, and burnish their anti-establishment credentials. This faction included the leadership of the United Auto Workers (which was dealing with an insurgency within its own ranks at the time), AFSCME (government workers), and several other liberal unions. These unions provided tens of millions of dollars to the UFW, and endorsed its pivotal grape boycott. Several liberal foundations also provided major donations. In fact, the UFW was soon getting more funding from outside groups than from its own members' dues.

The leadership of the worker elite was well aware that the ruling class regarded the farmworker cause as a credible threat. It had proven capable of mobilizing proletarians, oppressed nationalities, and radical activists across the country. But they calculated that, if properly harnessed, perhaps the farmworker struggle could instead be leveraged to extract concessions for the labor elite from the ruling class. They thought they could probably do business with Cesar Chavez. Worker elite leaders were confident that they could contain any revolutionary tendencies among the farmworkers by using financial purse strings or, if necessary, by playing their "ace in the hole": white supremacy and anti-immigrant nativism.

Eventually the "pro-UFW" section of the worker elite had its way. The UFW was brought into the mainstream and officially welcomed into the AFL-

Cesar Chavez, speaking at a United Farm Workers rally, June 1974.

48

CIO. (Recently, it quit to join the Change to Win coalition.) This "legitimization," which seemed impressive on the surface, actually facilitated the union's rapid decline as a social movement. The worker elite has its priorities, and proletarian insurgency isn't one of them.

Dramatic early victories against Western grape and lettuce growers gave way to rapid organizational and political collapse. Still potent as a symbol of Latino pride, and still taking in big donations, the UFW started to hollow out. It began to prioritize direct mail campaigns over struggle in the fields. It threw its energy into legislative battles and the election of liberal figures like Robert Kennedy. The UFW did win hundreds of union elections, but most of them never resulted in contract victories.

Cesar Chavez turned out to be a perfect vehicle for the worker elite. He deeply distrusted the motives, and questioned the abilities, of ordinary farmworkers. Seized by a messianic calling, he squashed all dissent and rank and file initiative within the union, and carried out vicious purges of experienced organizers who disagreed with his increasingly delusional edicts, as he finally degenerated into cultism and paranoia.

Moreover, counter to the carefully airbrushed mythology, Chavez repeatedly attacked and disparaged "wetbacks" and "illegals," inflicting devastating injuries to proletarian unity. In 1974, for instance, Chavez initiated a "Campaign Against Illegals," during which the union reported thousands of undocumented workers to the INS. The UFW even paid hundreds of vigilantes, who Chavez called the "wet line," to confront and stop undocumented immigrants. His views towards undocumented workers didn't start to change substantially until the 1980s, after repeated criticism from civil rights groups and a dawning recognition of "the demographic reality that most California farmworkers were undocumented."[60]

Chavez's authoritarian personality cult was both encouraged and appropriated by the leadership of the labor elite. AFL-CIO officials were happy to expand their reach

49

among Latino workers, but, like Chavez, they had no interest in allowing militant rank and file farmworkers to make their own decisions.

After Chavez's death in 1993, opportunists ran the UFW in typical AFL-CIO style:

> The union is now run by Cesar's son-in-law, Arturo Rodríquez.... Perhaps the word that best describes Rodríquez is incompetent; certainly he has shown none of the abilities of any of the great UFW organizers.
>
> He does appear to have a talent for overseeing, along with Cesar's son Paul and other family members and assorted scoundrels, an empire—begun by Chavez himself—of housing developments, radio stations, consulting enterprises, mass-mailing fund-raising campaigns, and marketing schemes (UFW paraphernalia, Chavez mementos, and the like). Meanwhile, pensions and health funds are awash in cash, but precious few workers get any benefits. In a labor movement notorious for corruption and shortchanging the membership, the United Farm Workers has secured a place on the union wall of infamy.[61]

The original UFW volunteer activists were famous for living frugally. They usually went without salaries altogether, surviving on meager expense payments and donated housing. Cesar Chavez, whatever his faults, lived an austere life. He carried out a series of highly publicized fasts. He was famous for never accepting more than $5,000 a year in salary.[62] Today National VP Armando Elenes gets total compensation of $126,307 a year for "leading" the union—whose membership is still proletarian, still poor, and still without significant political power.[63] "¡Sí Se Puede!", the battle slogan of the original United Farm Workers' Union, has become a registered federal trademark. It's "illegal" for it to be used without permission from UFW bureaucrats.

Things worked out well for the labor elite, and for the ruling class. A vibrant, dangerous proletarian movement was blunted, and came firmly under the control of a worker elite clique, which now has a death grip on the "offical" farmworker franchise. There are new, independent efforts to organize California farmworkers, but they have to step carefully around the institutional presence and mixed legacy of the UFW.

The worker elite's embrace of the UFW clearly had nothing to do with making revolution. In fact, it functioned to help forestall revolution. Still, even the treacherous breed of "assistance" the worker elite gave to proletarian farmworkers wasn't automatic. The UFW emerged at a time when anti-capitalist struggle around the world was at a high tide, causing the labor elite to triangulate its options carefully. In another period, they might easily have calculated differently. The Teamsters' instinctive reaction—violent antagonism—was hardly an aberration.

SAN DIEGO (May 5, 2012) Service members and civilians gather to watch the Lewis and Clark-class dry cargo ship USNS Cesar Chavez (T-AKE 14) be christened and launched at General Dynamics National Steel and Shipbuilding Company's shipyard in San Diego. The mission of the Cesar Chavez is to deliver food, ammunition, fuel, and other provisions to strike groups and other naval forces at sea.

CONTRADICTIONS WITH THE BOURGEOISIE

Our bourgeois rulers need the worker elite, but they don't necessarily like it. How much privilege to afford the worker elite is a constant source of debate within ruling circles. In general, capitalists spend as little of their wealth on other people's privilege as they need to. And, as we witness today, capitalists are eager to undermine worker elites when they are no longer useful.

The worker elite's mythology centers around its supposedly "heroic" struggle up into the middle class, battling against the greedy capitalists. The worker elite also likes to define itself as a champion of the underdog, holding the front line against the rich. This is a dishonest and self-serving narrative. In fact, the worker elite as a class embodies accommodation with the bourgeoisie and betrayal of the proletariat.

Nevertheless, worker elites do often arise initially from an environment of proletarian struggle against the ruling class. Depending on how fresh this struggle is, and how unresolved it is, worker elites may continue to have sharp conflicts with the bourgeoisie, and especially the bourgeoisie's more recalcitrant elements. Unionized Korean autoworkers are a good example: their current middle class standard of living is the result of years of tough labor battles, and the workers still carry forward a range of militant traditions and tactics in the face of employer push-back.

We have seen that the threat of proletarian struggle provides key leverage in the worker elite's contention with the ruling class. But there are other factors that determine which workers become part of the elite as well. Leverage may arise from a worker elite's entrenched access to choke-points or strategic sectors of the economy. One example is the longshore industry. Dockworkers in the US have retained their status at the top of the worker elite partly because of their ability to paralyze world trade through strategic job actions. Also, short term sectoral labor shortages or changes in technology may also help shape the worker elite, as the ruling class uses incentives to hurry workers into critical jobs. (This may be the case with English-language call center workers in India.) Workers in military industries are often required to have a particularly high level of loyalty to the ruling class, and are often privileged.

The worker elite isn't just a puppet of the ruling class, although it often acts that way. Once established as a separate class, the worker elite generates its own agenda like every other class. It usually functions as part of a broad coalition of classes led by the bourgeoisie. But the worker elite must periodically re-negotiate its status with capital, which can cause labor disputes and other social friction. The contradictions between the worker elite and the ruling class sometimes provide openings for revolutionary politics. Under certain conditions, parts of the worker elite may ally with the proletariat in its fight against capital. When this occurs, it is not because they are both "working class," but because of their own concrete and independent class interests.

The worker elite's origins and conditions of life are embodied in distinctive cultural and political characteristics. In times of conflict with the bourgeoisie, members of the worker elite have certain practical advantages in comparison to the other middle classes. Worker elites tend to be less sheltered than intellectuals, for instance, and their experience with danger or violence on the job can make them more combative than other privileged middle classes. Experience as wage workers in large socialized enterprises permits some sections of the worker elite to achieve higher levels of unity than other middle classes, and gives them intimate, daily familiarity with capitalist treachery and hypocrisy.

From a political point of view, the worker elite is neither more "hopeless" nor more "revolutionary" than other privileged middle classes. Everything depends on concrete conditions. Despite their underlying class commonalities, the politics of entrenched "white" worker elites in North America are not identical to the politics of new worker elites in Brazil or Indonesia. And individuals in the worker elite are certainly just as capable of class suicide as intellectuals or members of the other middle classes.

Specific sectors of the worker elite have heightened or multiple contradictions with capitalism. Oppressed nationality worker elites have deep hatred for oppressor nation chauvinism—depending on conditions, they may gravitate towards active national liberation movements. Women of the worker elite may find themselves attracted to the struggles of proletarian women, especially when confronted by misogynist fundamentalism and fascism.

Nevertheless, the labor elite is always looking to augment its privileges, and will routinely betray the proletariat to gain more. Besides, time and the relative comforts of middle class life tend to erode the worker elite's combativeness and rebelliousness.

For instance, third and fourth generation union dockworkers in the US are so privileged and so isolated from the proletariat that they have substituted wishful thinking for struggle. Despite ritualistic invocation of past battles and stylized chest-thumping, their unions now resemble exclusive clubs or fraternities more than fighting organizations. Even the idea of cynically using proletarians as potential "shock troops" has flown off their radar screen. Most dockworkers look down on proletarians working in and around the waterfront, ignoring or even opposing their struggles.

This is exemplified by the longshore unions' shameful, chauvinist, and strategically foolish lack of solidarity with thousands of rebellious immigrant waterfront truckers and thousands of other struggling proletarians in the logistical supply chain stretching inland from the ports.

Along with their fellow middle classes, the worker elite everywhere makes defense of privilege their top priority. They spin this as a matter of "fairness" in comparison to what the greedy capitalists have, a claim that masks its essential elitism in relation to the proletariat.

We are often lectured in the bourgeois media that the rise of middle classes is intrinsically "democratic." But this is demonstrably false. As capitalist mouthpiece Francis Fukuyama says, "Middle class people do not necessarily support democracy in principle: like everyone else they are self-interested actors who want to protect their property and position. In countries such as China and Thailand, many middle class people feel threatened by the redistributive demands of the poor and hence have lined up in support of authoritarian governments that protect their class interests."[64] We know, in fact, that settler states such as the US have depended on the institutionalization of mass settler middle classes to make widespread land theft, genocide, slavery, and colonialism possible. This is not democracy.

When the worker elite does choose to fight the ruling class, it's often for overtly reactionary causes. For example,

the South African worker elite conducted a militant populist struggle to help establish apartheid. ("Workers of the World, Unite and Fight for a White South Africa" was one of their slogans.) The first "union label" campaign in the US was mobilized for the purpose of freezing Chinese labor out of the cigar rolling industry in California.

When abandoned by "their" capitalists, failing worker elites generally embrace right-wing populism, including the scapegoating of proletarians and other oppressed people. We might wish that disintegrating worker elites would choose to unite with the proletariat in its violent, dangerous, underdog fight against capital. But this isn't what comes naturally. In practice, abandoned worker elites cling to their privileges as natural entitlements. There is an instinctual tendency to seek out the "traitors" who "stabbed them in the back," singling out immigrants, women, religious or national minorities, Jewish bankers and other "disloyal" types of capitalists as the cause of their problems.

Despite the wishful expectations of some radicals, people pushed out of the worker elite do not readily accept "demotion" into the proletariat. It's one thing for an established worker elite to use proletarians as shock troops for leverage. It's something else entirely for them to view themselves as proletarians when the ruling class decides to revoke their middle class status. The spontaneous, materially-based desire for a return of the old corrupt social contract, including its "traditional" patriarchal and patriotic ideology, is deeply rooted and hard to overcome.

This desire for the old privileges, and the accompanying narrative of betrayal, is ready fuel for fascism and other forms of reactionary populism. Hitler and Mussolini leveraged these impulses to attract and recruit workers whose economic prospects had been crushed by the Great Depression. In fact, much of Nazism's popularity came from its corrupt promise to raise "Aryan" workers out of the proletariat for good. The Nazis promised to build an imperial Reich on the backs of the labor of conquered and enslaved non-"Aryan" proletarians. The superprofits from that atrocity would be used to subsidize a rarified German parasitic worker elite.

Today, right-wing populists are moving into the vacuum left by the decline of labor elites (and their enfeebled Lefts) in the old metropolitan centers. Greece, where fascism was once defeated and deeply unpopular, is now confronted with the rapid rise of reactionary, nativist Golden Dawn insurgents, who feed on the resentment of the millions who are losing their middle class jobs and way of life. Right-wing populism is on the rise throughout Western Europe, responding to the destruction of the social contracts that gave life to the labor elites.

Neo-fascists and right-wing militias are developing bases in the US "rust belt," where the "white" worker elite has been left high and dry by de-industrialization, disinvestment, and decimated social benefits. Actually, right-wing populism has growing influence throughout the whole settler worker elite. This reactionary sentiment is an expression of the class's resentful mood as it contemplates a diminished future. Perhaps, as one astute bourgeois commentator suggested, "People of privilege will always risk their complete destruction rather than surrender any material part of their advantage."[65]

The worker elite is a mass class that has significant contradictions with capital. Therefore the proletariat can't rule out alliances with worker elites, nor can it concede the discarded members of the worker elite to the reactionaries. Revolutionaries should fight for their political allegiance, just as we do with other middle classes. But worker elites are heavily invested in their privileges. Effective political work with the labor elite can only occur where there is a proletarian movement offering a clear and viable alternative to what is offered by capitalists and fascists. Above all, the proletariat needs to have independent leadership and initiative within any political alliance that includes the worker elite. Flattering a failing worker elite with crocodile tears for its lost privileges—like the right-wing populists do—leads to disaster for proletarian forces.

INTELLECTUALS AND THE WORKER ELITE

The worker elite has a complicated relationship with middle class intellectuals. Both middle classes play a role in controlling the proletariat, but they do so in markedly different ways. While the worker elite confronts the proletariat mainly in the labor market and in mass politics, intellectuals affect the proletariat by generating ruling class theory, culture, and strategy. They also staff the institutions of bourgeois socialization, especially the education system.

In most social contexts, there is little love lost between these two classes. Middle class intellectuals tend to look down on all working class people, especially people who work with their hands. Intellectuals' default assumption is that their superior education somehow confers greater intelligence.

In return for intellectuals' disdain, the labor elite tends to consider intellectuals to be "educated fools," whose lack of "real world" experience makes them weak and impractical. They strongly resent intellectuals' undeserved social prestige, which is based on their access to educational privilege and tradition.

Still, middle class intellectuals and worker elites have a common interest in implementing and enforcing a gen-

erous social contract. And each class has characteristics that can be valuable to the other. As a result, with varying levels of awkwardness, they often join together in political coalitions and parties, including those of the reformist Left.

Intellectuals recognize that the worker elite has certain kinds of leverage over both the capitalists and the proletariat that they themselves lack. They are happy to share some of this leverage, and to give advice to the worker elite over how to wield it. A steady trickle of intellectuals seeks out staff jobs with worker elite labor organizations. This is considered a legitimate and relatively lucrative career path for a liberal or "progressive" intellectual. Some intellectuals are idealistically attracted to the proletariat, and attempt to approach it through the worker elite. This usually leaves them in a politically compromised position.

Meanwhile, the labor elite recognizes the value of intellectuals' research and writing skills, and their familiarity with capitalist superstructure. Intellectuals sometimes provide the worker elite with increased access to the levers of bourgeois government, culture, and education. Associating with intellectuals in labor or political organizations may even enhance upward social mobility for individuals from the labor elite, some of whom seek staff jobs in unions or a career outside the working class altogether.

REFORM AND THE WORKER ELITE

The ruling class continuously represses proletarian struggle, but this is not enough to maintain its power. It requires other modes of control as well.

When the proletariat succeeds in winning a battle, the ruling class counterattacks by trying to transform whatever reforms or concessions they were forced to make into circumscribed, restricted privileges. The bourgeoisie thus undermines the revolutionary potential of the proletariat's partial victories. Restricting them diminishes a reform's overall cost, naturally. But even more important, the ruling class resumes control by selecting who the reform is "awarded" to. This reformist dynamic is what leads to the creation of many worker elites, and it is also vital to maintaining or extending their privileges. It's no surprise, then, that worker elites eagerly cooperate with the ruling class throughout the process of poisoning new reforms.

In rationalizing its corrupt arrangements with the bourgeoisie, the worker elite falsely portrays itself as the vanguard of the whole working class. It claims to be consolidating advanced reforms that will eventually trickle down to the proletariat. In fact, the worker elite cares first and foremost about its own class, and characteristically turns its back on the proletariat once it gets what it wants.

For instance, one of the great reform movements of the early labor movement in the US was the struggle for the 8-hour day. This demand galvanized millions of impoverished workers, who fought and sometimes died trying to attain it. (The Haymarket Massacre, and the tradition of May Day, started with the vicious repression of a rally in support of a strike for the 8-hour day in Chicago on May 4, 1886.) However, when 8-hour legislation was finally passed by the US congress in 1937 in response to this struggle, it turned out that it applied to a mere 20% of the workforce. Agricultural workers, most service workers, undocumented immigrants, and domestic workers—employment categories where oppressed nationality workers and women were heavily concentrated—were completely excluded from its provisions. This essentially turned the 8-hour day reform into an attack on the proletariat. Yet that fact somehow failed to keep the attention of the emerging "white" worker elite.

The excluded majority of workers were solemnly promised that this was just the beginning—soon everybody would win the 8-hour day. As we know, that never happened. Over time, more and more exclusions from the US 8-hour day were carved out. (More are being discussed right now in Congress.) Most of the proletariat never got anything from this reform, inside or outside the US. Unlike elite workers, proletarians in the factories still routinely work 10- and 12-hour shifts, six or seven days a week, usually without overtime pay. Farm laborers in the US often work 14- or 15-hour days.[66] Domestic work continues to be virtually endless.

What happened to the 8-hour day was ultimately a defeat for the proletariat. That isn't to say that the struggle for the 8-hour day couldn't be a legitimate struggle, either back in the 19th century or in our time. But when reforms are corraled and tailored for the benefit of an elite, leaving others behind, they are lost to the proletariat. What starts as a step out of oppression becomes a privilege: an actual fortification of bourgeois power.

Reforms can't be identified as "bourgeois" or "revolutionary" according to any programmatic formula. There's no universal checklist of characteristics that make a reform inherently good or bad. A given reform may beat back oppression, lift the proletariat out of slavery and starvation or enhance its unity and combative capacity. But the exact same reform, employed to create a worker elite or to entrench that elite's privileges, becomes an attack on the proletariat. The fundamental issue at stake in any reform is a basic question of class politics—who controls and benefits from it.

UNIONS AND THE WORKER ELITE

Trade unionism often accompanies the rise of worker elites. In fact, union membership is a typical badge of worker elite status. Every day in every part of the world, worker elite unions negotiate corrupt deals with capital and trash the interests of the proletariat. The worker elite is famous for its unions' clannish protectiveness, chauvinism, and parochial unwillingness to share power with other social forces. Many unions have been taken over by organized crime or reactionary governments. All in all it's understandable that many revolutionaries view unions with suspicion.

But treating unions as inherently reactionary is a serious mistake. The modern proletariat requires unions as weapons of struggle. In the hands of proletarians, unions are tactical necessities, crucial schools of class war, and reservoirs of class power.

On the most basic level, a union is an organization that strengthens the fight against capitalist employers by restraining competition among the workers. In that sense it is a limited, concrete expression of worker solidarity.

Yet as these notes insist, there are different classes of workers, different kinds of solidarity, and different kinds of struggle against the employers. Proletarians can use unions to fight oppression, to strengthen their unity and combative power. Worker elites can use unions to achieve and solidify privilege. Some unions are led by revolutionaries, some by fascists and gangsters, some by liberals. One union may attack immigrants, another may shelter a guerrilla army. All these differences are political, but at the most basic level they reflect differing class agendas.

It is exactly because of their persistent strategic and tactical significance that unions are a universal battleground between the proletariat and the worker elite. A worker elite that can't control a country's overall labor movement has failed to live up to its social contract with the bourgeoisie. From a revolutionary perspective, proletarian unions dominated by the worker elite are destined to fail the class.

The worker elite has its own unions, yet it also attempts to take over proletarian unions, from above and within. As part of this effort, the worker elite offers to buy off the leadership of proletarian unions, tempting activists with middle class staff jobs, mainstream prestige, immunity from repression, and other privileges. It constantly maneuvers to co-opt proletarian struggles and blunt their radical edge.

Worker elite leadership, characteristically opportunist, is vulnerable to the manipulations of organized crime and state agents. The worker elite does not hesitate to violently destroy proletarian unions either. A prime example is the American Institute for Free Labor Development (AIFLD), the AFL-CIO's murderous and long-lasting counterinsurgency program, funded with worker elite union dues and carefully guided by the US State Department and CIA.[67]

The proletariat's fight for leadership of its own class's labor movement is one of its greatest challenges. The proletariat must defeat the hegemony of the worker elite's organizations, and battle to control its own. It must also fight off the infiltration of racketeers and other lumpen forces. This multi-faceted struggle will only be successful if it is understood as a deep conflict among distinct classes with different material interests, rather than as just an abstract question of program, political line or ideology.

FREE LABOR WILL WIN

CASE STUDY: AUTO ASSEMBLY WORKERS

Worker elites and cars seem to go hand in hand. Not just because one buys the other, but because there is a recurring historical pattern of autoworkers being elevated out of the proletariat.[68] This phenomenon is partly explained by the vulnerable nature of auto production, with its complex supply chains and manufacturing choke points. Also, since auto assembly is a capital intensive process, wages are a relatively small percentage of overall costs for the capitalists.

But beyond economic expediency, the link between the auto industry and privilege has its own historical continuity, as well. Unsurprisingly, this is a relentlessly male history and culture. Women have been virtually excluded from auto assembly lines all over the world, sometimes under the pretext of "protective" legislation prohibiting women from working night shifts or accepting overtime.

In 1914, Henry Ford made the shocking announcement that he would start paying auto assembly workers $5 a day, roughly doubling the prevailing autoworker wage in the US. (Part of this wage was technically a bonus. To get it, workers had to prove—to a so-called "Socialization Organization"—that they were living their lives "the American Way.") Ford also reduced the work day from nine to eight hours. For him this wasn't charity, nor was it primarily a concession to organized proletarian militancy, although the threat of the IWW was in the background. Ford was looking at a bigger picture, trying to literally create a better class of worker.

He had his reasons. His new assembly lines were grueling, monotonous, and easily sabotaged. Even ordinary worker absenteeism could be devastating to his profits. What he needed was a group of loyal, dependable workers, with low attrition rates. And he had another motive: "Ford had reasoned that since it was now possible to build inexpensive cars in volume, more of them could be sold if employees could afford to buy them. The $5 day... contributed to the emergence of the American middle class."[69]

Ford's idea of middle class workers was thoroughly patriarchal. The few women hired by the company—mostly in the offices—were fired immediately if it was discovered that they were married to a man with a job.

> Ford believed that only a specific form of family relationship—one in which the husband provided for a non-income-earning wife—would insure the stability of his labor force. The Five Dollar Day would encourage this type of family, in which a male wage supported a dependent family, who would then have no need to use their homes to make money. Ford appeared to sanction only the most "middle-class" form of family life, or what seemed to be the middle-class form of life to him, where a husband earned enough to protect the home as a sanctuary and a refuge.[70]

Autoworkers in the US were early to unionize, and they played a key role in forging and policing the New Deal social contract. One of the pivotal labor battles of the 1930s was the Flint sit-down strike against General Motors. But "white" autoworker militancy didn't extend to solidarity with oppressed nationality workers. As J. Sakai documents, the first autoworker contracts after the sit-down strikes made it literally illegal for Black workers to get jobs on the assembly line. In fact, they were trapped in inferior jani-

Henry Ford, 1927 (left);
Autoworkers' houses. Flint, Michigan, 1937 (right).

tor or foundry jobs. Job segregation continued to be a hallmark of the unionized industry for decades. Well into the 1940s the Atlanta UAW remained all "white."[71] Segregation continued in union plants into the 1970s.[72]

During World War II, a small cohort of women was hired to work on US auto assembly lines to replace men drafted into the military. After the war, they were immediately replaced by men.

In the 1960s and 70s, Detroit was the site of a major insurgency by Black autoworkers, who revolted against brutal working conditions and flagrant discrimination in the plants.[73] This struggle forced the capitalists to make major concessions. These concessions played a role not only in desegregating the assembly plants, but in establishing a modern African American worker elite. In its aftermath, "life was good for blacks [sic] who were able to hold onto their assembly line jobs. Steadily employed black auto workers made enough money to buy their own homes, to put away money for retirement, to own their own cars, and even to send their children to college."[74]

Autoworker jobs also became linked with the rise of worker elites in Western Europe in the post-WWII period, although in some places (like Italy's Fiat plants) this development was still in doubt as late as the 1970s. As auto plants opened in Japan, and then other parts of Asia, the pattern of autoworker elites continued.

Toyota and other Japanese auto companies developed an elaborate system of corporate

Cadillac, USA 1973

paternalism to ensure (all-male) assembly worker loyalty and to buy labor peace. Besides high seniority-based wages and generous pensions, this system included assurances of a lifetime job, inexpensive company housing, extra money for each child, and special deals on buying homes, cars, and expensive restaurant meals. Team spirit was promoted through corporate outings, group drinking binges, shop-floor calisthenics, and company songs. Managers visited workers' homes and hospital rooms. There were special facilities set aside for worker hobbies and other leisure activities. One Japanese politician remarked that elite Japanese workers "are owned like pets by their companies." Their perks, he said, were "like dog food." Although this paternalistic system has weakened in recent decades, its legacy continues in the Japanese-owned auto plants all over the world.[75]

Immediately after the Korean War ended in 1953, foreign capitalists moved to transform South Korea into an industrial export platform, slamming its economy abruptly into the world commodity market. The Korean economy was dominated by a small group of conglomerates (chaebols), heavily funded by Japanese and Western capital and protected by a vicious right-wing dictatorship. Workers responded with an inspiring upsurge of militant resistance, fighting pitched battles with police and soldiers. But the ruling class was eventually able to curtail this rebellion using a combination of brutal terror, massive infusions of capital, and reform legislation. A key element allowing the capitalists to regain solid control was the formation of a worker elite, rooted in important industries, like auto. Groups of industrial workers were rapidly pulled up out of the proletariat.

Today income inequality among workers is a notable feature of the Korean economic landscape. "Among developed countries, Korea has one of the biggest gaps in wages and welfare between the top and bottom 10 percent of workers," according to Bae Kyu-shik, a researcher at the Korea Labour Institute.[76]

Currently, Korea makes 40% of all General Motors cars; Hyundai and Kia have become automotive giants. Korean auto assembly workers work long hours. And they still have a reputation for struggling hard against corporate attacks, including a current wave of casualization. But the terms of conflict have changed dramatically. The workers are now

HIGH LEVEL TALKS

This past May, Moon Jin-koo of the Federation of Korea Trade Unions, South Korea's largest union federation, accompanied Korean President Park Geun-hye and several corporate leaders on a trip to the US. It was what Moon called a "united front" to encourage foreign investment on the peninsula. Dashing their hopes, however, the delegation was blindsided by a firestorm of criticism from US business executives, who demanded that action be taken immediately to lower wages at the Korean auto plants. GM CEO Daniel Akerson confirmed the company's desire to invest $8 billion more in Korea, but he simultaneously threatened to pull out of Korea completely if wages weren't brought back in line.[77]

"'We are upset by his remarks,' said FKTU spokesman Choi Jong-hak. 'We did not go all the way to the US to hear that.'... Choi said Akerson's comments on a potential shift of production was an empty threat to tame the union ahead of [contract] talks...."[78]

Hyundai, South Korea 2006

defending elite jobs. The union wage is about PPP $40,000, including lots of overtime pay, family supplements, and bonuses. It has shot up rapidly in the last several years.

Brazilian autoworkers, overwhelmingly male, have moved rapidly into the middle class, and, as mentioned above, play an important part in the PT political regime. Current wages for assembly are around PPP $31,000. Car production has also been ramping up in Mexico, and it seems to be following a familiar script.

> "The Mexican worker is a natural craftsman, and global investors are showing their confidence in Mexican labor," said Alberto Rabago, a union official who started working for Chrysler in 1959 as a floor sweeper when the company made Mexican versions of its DeSoto and Plymouth sedans for the local market.
>
> Now Chrysler makes its muscular Hemi engines at the Saltillo Motors plant here in the deserts south of Texas. At another Chrysler plant nearby, $35,000 Ram pickups fly off the assembly line at a rate of one every 80 seconds…
>
> Overall, Mexico is making nearly 3 million vehicles a year, with output expected to increase 38 percent by 2016 as Nissan, Mazda and Audi add new plants and other manufacturers ramp up production. GM said last week it will invest $691 million to boost its Mexican assembly lines.[79]

This is taking place in a country where male industrial workers—miners, oilfield workers, steelworkers, railway workers—have historically been treated as "labor aristocrats." At one time union workers got special social benefits and had their own system of exclusive parks and resorts. The dominant manufacturing unions have long been an integral part of a syndicalist political structure, closely tied to the main political parties and the government.[80]

Work on the auto assembly lines and in the heavy machine shops is considered a male province. Women do work in the Mexican auto parts and supply factories, but even there they are employed in significantly lower proportions than in other manufacturing industries. (Women workers' pay is about 25% lower than men's, just like in the US.)[81]

Today, the average auto assembly wage in Mexico is about PPP $18,000—much less than in the US, Japan, Europe or Korea. Yet this is more than twice the wage of Mexican garment workers (PPP $8,000); it is eight times the national minimum wage (PPP $2,253).

> *AGUASCALIENTES, Mexico — For 12 hours, Luis Moreno moved camshafts along the assembly line at the vast Nissan plant here, 30 seconds for each one. Now he was coming home in the dark, just as he'd left. His five children were waiting inside. His wife. Her parents.*
>
> *"I want you to know something," said Moreno, 31, outside the small house he bought last year with a mortgage financed by Nissan. "It might sound sentimental or corny. But this company has given me everything."*
>
> *…Here in central Mexico, where the global auto industry is booming, a job at Nissan is a path to the middle class. To work for the company in Aguascalientes today is akin to what it might have been like working in the 1950s for General Motors in Flint, Mich., or for Ford in Dearborn….*
>
> *[Mr. Moreno's] wife is a homemaker. Their entire family is covered by a company-subsidized health insurance policy that costs the equivalent of $4 a week. Next year, Moreno—the son of a day laborer—thinks he will buy his first car, a Nissan, with a loan financed by the company. The mortgage on the family's $27,000 home is $210 a month, deducted automatically from his Nissan paycheck.*

And Moreno says these are not the benefits that have made the biggest difference in his life, the things that have "changed him." Nissan has given him classes in ethics, health and good hygiene. It has steeped him in Japanese corporate concepts, promoted on posters throughout the sprawling plant, with slogans such as "Kaizen" ("continuous improvement") and "NPW" ("Nissan Production Way") that Moreno has come to view as metaphors for life....

....After 17 years processing engine blocks as a machinist, Ruben Flores, 47, makes just $160 a week [note: not PPP adjusted for cost of living]. Still, he owns a five-bedroom house, a Nissan Frontier pickup and a Nissan Altima sedan, and his two children are on track for professional degrees.

"My son is studying to be an engineer," Flores said proudly, standing by his car in the employee parking lot after his shift, which went from 7am to 7pm. He looked up at the plant, its long, squat buildings buzzing with a low hum. "He'll go straight in there the day he graduates."[82]

What Mr. Moreno told the reporter is revealing: it isn't just relatively high wages that have "changed" him. It's a constellation of economic, social, and political factors. It's a wife at home, medical insurance, a car, a new culture.

Volkswagen de México

MORE THAN JUST WAGES

Meanwhile, as the autoworkers put in their shifts at the Nissan factory, 12 tiring hours at a time, tens of thousands of their compatriots are trekking north to labor in the fields of US agribusiness. Many are Indigenous, about 28% are women, some are children. The trip is arduous; quite a few have no legal documents and face significant risks just crossing the border—prison, robbery, rape, and even death from heat stroke and dehydration in the Sonoran Desert.

In the course of a year, the average migrant farmworker family doesn't make that much less than those of Moreno, Flores, and their fellow autoworkers. At least some migrant farmworker families could achieve income above the global "middle class" PPP $10-15,000 data point. Are they part of the worker elite?

Clearly not. Migrant farmworkers' lives are completely different from those of the autoworkers. They have little job security and few benefits. Their work is dangerous and back-breaking, with constant exposure to blazing sun and toxic fertilizers. They have almost no political influence except what they can generate through their own struggle and solidarity. It's difficult for them to keep their families in one place; many leave their loved ones back in Mexico while they work. Their future in society is uncertain. Instead of relative prestige, they routinely face discrimination, sexual harassment, and racist insults. This is not a recipe for a worker elite.

The contrast between the Mexican Nissan workers and Mexican migrant farmworkers shows that privilege flows along multiple pathways—a mix of income, location, political status, gender, nationality, and historical circumstance. It's a classic illustration of why we need to make a holistic analysis of worker elites.

Chinese autoworkers are now facing direct competition with Mexican autoworkers, as labor costs in the two countries converge. The Chinese auto industry is heavily subsidized by the government, which has named it a "pillar industry." Pay is well above what most manufacturing workers make and is going up rapidly. One automaker in China saw wages in their plants rise from PPP $7,270 in 2003 to PPP $14,540 in 2010.[83]

Autoworkers are watched over by paternalistic unions. Union representatives sometimes double as factory managers.

> *In the core factories, the official All-China Federation of Trade Unions (ACFTU) has an extensive bureaucracy that administers the companies' generous welfare programs and acts as a consultant to management on wages and working conditions (there are no collective bargaining agreements). In most of the suppliers, unions don't exist at all, or they have been installed on behalf of local government labor bureaus, Communist Party chiefs, or managers.[84]*

In 2010, strikes at several Chinese auto plants were settled with raises of 20–50%. These were hard fought struggles, even featuring occasional battles with company goons and insubordination against company unions. Yet the strike wave occurred in an interesting political and economic context:

> *While Honda and Toyota suffered tremendous profit losses thanks to the strikes, in this instance Chinese autoworker demands for increased wages inadvertently converged with the aims of the central government. The CCP's 12th Fifth Year Plan (2011–2015)… recognizes the importance of raising wages as a share of GDP. If China's economy continues to grow at current levels of investment, her production capacity will eventually outstrip global demand. Thus, it is*

necessary for China to move from an export driven
economy to a more balanced model based on greater
domestic consumption. Wages will play a key role in
helping to increase this consumption…. While work-
ers were in no way manipulated by the CCP to go
on strike, their calls for partaking in a greater share
of the wealth were no doubt met with sympathy by
certain factions within the government."[85]

To round out this discussion of autoworkers and the worker
elite, two bar graphs are reproduced below. The first shows
average auto wages; the second average textile wages:

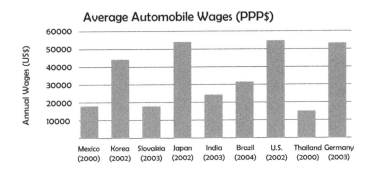

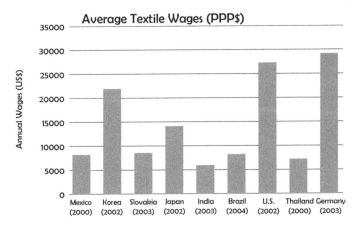

Note that these charts had to be drawn to different scales;
auto assembly workers and textile workers exist, literally, in
different wage universes.[86]

CONCLUSION

The worker elite—a small minority of workers—continuously attacks, restricts, and undermines the proletariat's struggle for freedom. The predominantly reactionary role of this privileged class flows directly from its material interests. The worker elite's hegemony over the proletariat, deeply rooted in maleness and multiple forms of chauvinism, is persistent and strong. Generations of revolutionaries have been unable to dislodge it politically or practically. In the meantime, privilege continues to evolve and gain sophistication, as worker elites become increasingly flexible and transnational.

Privilege within the working class prevents us from overthrowing capitalism. There's no point in pretending that the worker elite is a leading protagonist of revolution, and then scratching our heads when reforms somehow keep mysteriously degenerating into anti-proletarian systems of privilege. And what kind of "working class politics" is it that permits a giant proletariat centered around women to be "represented" by a thin layer of worker elite men?

Revolution requires us to break the worker elite's death grip on the proletariat (and on the Left). The parasitic and patriarchal agenda of this class must be defeated. Eventually, the worker elite must be dissolved.

Class struggle is going on every day inside the working class. It's time to choose where our class loyalty lies—with the proletariat or with its minders in the worker elite.

Construction workers, Tibet.

NOTES:

1. The traditional names for these classes are antiquated, and have become burdened with considerable baggage over time. In particular, the term "labor aristocracy" has tended to limit discussion of privilege within the working class, focussing on a handful of trade union officials and bureaucrats. These notes use "worker elite" to denote a mass class.

2. "Criminal" is used here mainly as a practical description, not a moral judgment. The lumpen is a product of extreme social pressures. On an institutional level, the bourgeoisie uses, organizes and profits from criminality. And the borders of criminality shift as the needs of capitalism change. On an individual level, many lumpen would certainly prefer to have a steady job—or for that matter, a place in a revolutionary army. Neither of these is readily available in most places right now. From the point of view of the proletariat, the agents of repression are also criminals. Their "job" is intimidation, occupation, imprisonment, war crimes, genocide, and violent defense of the rich.

3. These notes do not directly address the ongoing debate about whether or not a worker elite/labor aristocracy even exists. This question should be considered settled after over 150 years of theory and practice by leading revolutionaries. For those still in doubt, two readings are suggested: 1) J. Sakai's brilliant *Settlers: The Mythology of the White Proletariat* (Morningstar Press, 1989), a new edition of which is being released by Kersplebedeb and PM Press in 2014. This underground classic is a devastating and well-researched attack on what is perhaps the iconic worker elite—the socially bribed "white" working class in the US—as well as on its apologists. 2) Zak Cope's recent *Divided World, Divided Class: Global Political Economy and the Stratification of Labour Under Capitalism* (Kersplebedeb, 2012). This book provides a convincing historical narrative of the rise of worker elites in tandem with colonialism. Cope also attempts to quantify the economic discrepancies between the labor aristocracy/elite and the proletariat. The latter effort is perhaps less convincing, but nevertheless presents overwhelming evidence of the economic disparities between workers of the poorer and richer countries.

4. Sakai, *Settlers* (1989), p. 83 (p. 188 in 2014 edition).

5. Franklin Roosevelt, State of the Union Address, January 3, 1938 (http://www.let.rug.nl/usa/presidents/franklin-delano-roosevelt/state-of-the-union-1938.php).

6. For more on the central role of women in the proletariat, see the author's *Exodus and Reconstruction: Working-Class Women at the Heart of Globalization* (Kersplebedeb, 2012). The gendered character of class is a theme that runs through the theoretical work of Butch Lee. See, for example, *Night-Vision: Illuminating War and Class on the Neo-Colonial Terrain* (with Red Rover, Vagabond, 1993) and *The Military Strategy of Women and Children* (Kersplebedeb, 2003).

7. Purchasing power parity is a potent tool, but still imprecise. The World Bank was heavily criticized for its earliest PPP calculations, which were skewed by a bias towards the (higher) cost of living in big cities. The newer version is still an approximation, since cost of living varies substantially from region to region within countries. Any cost of living comparison requires choosing a "basket" of goods and services to compare, which is difficult to do without introducing biases based on income level and cultural difference. Wages and inflation sometimes change rapidly. Nevertheless, PPP comparisons, with all their drawbacks, provide much more useful information than was available previously.

8. "Modern Slavery Statistics," Abolition Media (http://abolitionmedia.org/about-us/modern-slavery-statistics).

9. *The Economist*, March 3, 2012 (http://www.economist.com/node/21548963).

10. Ibid.

11. Gabriel Thompson, "Could You Survive on $2 a Day?" *Mother Jones*, December 13, 2012 (http://www.motherjones.com/politics/2012/12/extreme-poverty-unemployment-recession-economy-fresno).

12. Howard Schneider, "This is why the textile industry is relocating to places like Bangladesh," *Washington Post*, July 12, 2013 (http://www.washingtonpost.com/blogs/wonkblog/wp/2013/07/12/this-is-why-the-textile-industry-is-relocating-to-places-like-bangladesh).

13. *China Labour Bulletin*, June 10, 2013 (http://www.clb.org.hk/en/content/wages-china).

14. Thompson, op. cit.

15. "Poverty Facts and Stats," *Global Issues*, January 7, 2013 (http://www.globalissues.org/article/26/poverty-facts-and-stats).

16. US Department of Health and Human Services, 2008 (http://aspe.hhs.gov/hsp/indicators08/apa.shtml#ftanf2).

17. International Labor Organization, "Is it the end of a low-wage production model in China?" December 14, 2012 (http://www.ilo.org/global/about-the-ilo/newsroom/news/WCMS_192956/lang—en/index.htm).

18. Wage Indicator 2010–2012, IMF World Economic Outlook Database, April 2012; *The Economist*, January, 2012, reported at http://www.paywizard.co.uk/main/pay/global-wage-comparison

19. US Census Bureau, "Preliminary Estimate of Weighted Average Poverty Thresholds for 2012" (http://www.census.gov/hhes/www/poverty/data/threshld) and Associated Press, "U.S. sees highest poverty spike since the 1960s, leaving 50 million Americans poor as government cuts billions in spending… so does that mean there's no way out?" *Daily Mail*, July 24, 2013 (http://www.dailymail.co.uk/news/article-2302997/U-S-sees-highest-poverty-spike-1960s-leaving-50-million-Americans-poor-government-cuts-billions-spending.html). This is a pre-tax figure; in practice, people at this income level pay little or no income tax.

20. http://koreaconsulting.blogspot.com/2012/07/s-koreas-monthly-minimum-wage-to-top.html

21. "Chinese Factories Turn to Outsourced Workers," *Want China Times*, March 18, 2013 (http://www.wantchinatimes.com/news-subclass-cnt.aspx?id=20130318000020&cid=1102).

22. *Gurgaon Workers News* gives 20,000 rupees a month as a typical call center wage in 2012. This is the equivalent of PPP $12,456 according to ILO calculations (http://gurgaonworkersnews.wordpress.com/page/2/). Other sources fall in the same range. For instance, James and Vira, "'Unionising' the New Spaces of the Economy? Alternative Labour Organizing in India's IT Enabled

Services-Business Process Outsourcing Industry," *Geoforum*, October 26, 2009, p. 6.; also Paul Glader, "As Indian Companies Grow in the US, Outsourcing Comes Home," *Washington Post*, May 20, 2011 (http://www.washingtonpost.com/business/as-indian-companies-grow-in-the-us-outsourcing-comeshome/2011/05/17/AFZbrp7G_story.html).

23. Edward Niedermeyer, "Is China's Cheap Labor a Thing of the Past?" *The Truth About Cars*, September 29, 2011, p. 1. (http://www.thetruthaboutcars.com/2011/09/is-chinas-cheap-labor-a-thing-of-the-past)

24. US Department of Labor, "Changing Characteristics of US Farm Workers: 21 Years of Findings from the National Agricultural Workers Survey," May 12, 2011 (http://migrationfiles.ucdavis.edu/uploads/cf/files/2011-may/carroll-changing-characteristics.pdf). Average farmworker family income, from all sources is listed as $17,500–$20,000; approximate income tax has been subtracted. Many farm workers make gross wages of $6,000 or less.

25. *Want China Times*, op. cit.

26. "Meatpacking in the US: Still a 'Jungle' Out There?" *PBS Now*, December 15, 2006. This citation gives a pre-tax figure of about $23,000. Tax has been roughly calculated at 20% (http://www.pbs.org/now/shows/250/meat-packing.html).

27. US Department of Commerce, "Manufacturing Biweekly Update," December 7, 2012 (http://www.trade.gov/mas/ian/mbu). This source lists a full-time gross income of about $38,400. 20% has been subtracted to approximate taxes.

28. Timothy James Kerswell, *The Global Division of Labour and the Division in Global Labour* (Queensland University of Technology, 2011), "Average Automobile Wages,"p. 49.

29. US Bureau of Labor Statistics (http://www.healthcare-salaries.com/technicians/x-ray-technician-salary). Average gross salary of $56,000, minus 20% taxes.

30. Want ads, CATHO (http://emprego.catho.com.br/vagas/manutencao).

31. Kerswell, op. cit. p. 49.

32. Alan Feuer, "On the Waterfront, Rise of the Machines," *New York Times*, September 28, 2012. Also John Gillie, "80 Tacoma Longshore Workers Get Boost into Regular Union Ranks," *The News Tribune*, December 25, 2012 (http://www.thenewstribune. com/2012/12/25/2413972/80-tacoma-longshore-workers-get. html).

33. Kerswell, op. cit. p. 49.

34. (http://www.irinnews.org/report/96073/zambia-dreaming-of-a-minimum-wage)

35. "Zambia Seizes Control of Chinese-Owned Mine Amid Safety Fears," *BBC*, February 20, 2013 (http://www.bbc.co.uk/news/business-21520478).

36. Kerswell, op. cit.

37. US Census Bureau, 2012.

38. Tom Orlik, Sophia Chen, "New Survey Finds China Unequal, Unemployed and Untrusting," *Wall Street Journal*, July 26, 2013.

39. See, for instance, Zak Cope, *Divided World, Divided Class*, referenced above.

40. For instance, some mainstream economists have proposed PPP $12 to $50 a day as a middle class income (Milanovic and Yitzhaki); others prefer a relative figure: 75% to 125% of each country's median income (Birdsall, Graham and Pettinato). In 2012, the Brazilian government proudly announced that more than half the national population was now "middle class." They were referring to what is known in that country as the "C class," a group with income of 291–1019 reales a month—roughly PPP $2,040–$7,152 a year! (Low as that range may be, the government, and many economists, were able to identify large increases in consumption from this sector.)

41. Homi Kharas, "The Emerging Middle Class in Developing Countries," OECD Development Centre, Working Paper 285, January 2010.

42. Nancy Birdsall, Christian Meyer, "Oops: Economists in Confused Search for the Middle Class in the Developing World," Center for Global Development, May 31, 2012. (http://www.cgdev.org/blog/oops-economists-confused-search-middle-class-developing-world)

43. Nancy Birdsall, "A Note on the Middle Class in Latin America," Working Paper 303, Center for Global Development, August 2012, p. 4 (http://www.cgdev.org/files/1426386_file_Birsdall_Note_on_Middle_Class_FINAL.pdf).

44. World Bank, "In Brazil, an Emergent Middle Class Takes Off," November 13, 2012 (http://www.worldbank.org/en/news/feature/2012/11/13/middle-class-in-Brazil-Latin-America-report).

45. Shimelse Ali, Uri Dadush, "The Global Middle Class is Bigger Than We Thought," *Foreign Policy*, May 16, 2012 (http://www.foreignpolicy.com/articles/2012/05/16/the_global_middle_class_is_bigger_than_we_thought?page=0,1).

46. Diana Farrell, Eric Beinhocker, "Next Big Spenders: India's Middle Class," McKinsey Global Institute, May 19, 2007 (http://www.mckinsey.com/Insights/MGI/In_the_news/Next_big_spenders_Indian_middle_class).

47. Homi Kharas, op. cit.

48. David Court, Laxman Narasimhan, "Capturing the World's Emerging Middle Class," McKinsey & Company, July 2010. "Developing countries" for the purposes of this study are: Argentina, Brazil, Chile, China, Colombia, Egypt, India, Indonesia, Iran, Malaysia, Mexico, Nigeria, Pakistan, Peru, the Philippines, Poland, Romania, Russia, South Africa, Thailand, Turkey, Ukraine, Venezuela, and Vietnam (http://www.mckinsey.com/insights/consumer_and_retail/capturing_the_worlds_emerging_middle_class).

49. Satyananda J. Gabriel, *Chinese Capitalism and the Modernist Vision* (Psychology Press, 2006), p. 77.

50. "Global Trade Liberalization and the Developing Countries," International Monetary Fund, November 2001 (http://www.imf.org/external/np/exr/ib/2001/110801.htm).

51. Homi Kharas, op. cit.

52. Mario Pazzini, "An Emerging Middle Class," *OECD Observer*, 2012. (http://www.oecdobserver.org/news/fullstory.php/aid/3681/An_emerging_middle_class.html)

53. ILO Global Wage Report 2012/13, p. i.

54. Homi Kharas, op. cit.

55. Gino Pepi, "Brazil: Born to be Empire," *International Left Review*, August 1, 2013 (http://internationalleftreview.com/brazil-born-to-be-empire).

56. Arthur Brice, "Brazil Enacts Racial Discrimination Law, But Some Say It's Not Needed," CNN, July 21, 2010.

57. Pepi, op. cit. (http://internationalleftreview.com/?p=87).

58. Andrew Marantz, "My Summer at an Indian Call Center," *Mother Jones*, August 2011. (http://www.motherjones.com/politics/2011/05/indian-call-center-americanization) See also, Kolinko, "Ten Years After and a Global Crisis Later; Preface to Indian Edition 2011," *Gurgaon Workers News* #58, August/September 2013 (http://gurgaonworkersnews.wordpress.com).

59. Ibid. Kolinko, quoting *Financial Times*, May 20, 2011.

60. For documentation, see Justin Feldman, "Reinventing Cesar Chavez," *CounterPunch*, April 3, 2013 (http://www.counterpunch.org/2013/04/03/reinventing-cesar-chavez).

61. Michael D. Yates, "The Rise and Fall of the United Farm Workers," *Monthly Review*, August 23, 2013 (http://monthlyreview.org/2010/05/01/the-rise-and-fall-of-the-united-farm-workers).

62. "The Story of Cesar Chavez," United Farm Workers website (http://www.ufw.org/_page.php?inc=history/07.html&menu=research).

63. Union Facts, (http://www.unionfacts.com/employees/United_Farm_Workers)

64. Francis Fukuyama, "The Future of History: Can Liberal Democracy Survive the Decline of the Middle Class?" *Foreign Affairs*, January/February 2012 (http://www.viet-studies.info/kinhte/FA_FutureOfHistory_Fukuyama.htm).

65. John Kenneth Galbraith, *The Age of Uncertainty* (BBC, 1977), p. 22.

66. Sharon Sullivan, "Early-Season Crop Freeze Affects Migrant Workers as Well as Farmers," *Post Independent,* July 12, 2013 (http://www.postindependent.com/news/grandjunction/7248381-113/tamales-workers-farm-center).

67. See, for instance, Kim Scipes, *AFL-CIO's Secret War Against Developing Country Workers: Solidarity or Sabotage?* (Lexington Books, 2011).

68. There is usually a sharp distinction, in terms of pay, benefits, working conditions and demographics, between two sectors of auto industry workers. The "core" employees on assembly lines, in engine plants and key machine shops are usually treated very favorably in comparison with "supplier" workers who manufacture auto electronics, batteries, hardware, and small parts, often working for subcontractors.

69. "Henry Ford's $5-a-Day Revolution," Ford Motor Company press release (http://corporate.ford.com/news-center/press-releases-detail/677-5-dollar-a-day). Also, "The Assembly Line and the $5 Day—Background Reading," Michigan Department of Natural Resources (http://www.michigan.gov/dnr/0,1607,7-153-54463_18670_18793-53441—,00.html).

70. Martha May, "The Historical Problem of the Family Wage: The Ford Motor Company and the Five Dollar Day," *Feminist Studies,* Vol. 8, No. 2, Summer, 1982 (http://www.jstor.org/stable/3177569).

71. Sakai, op. cit., pp. 87–88 (pages 198–201 in 2014 edition).

72. See, for instance, Kevin Boyle, *The UAW and the Heyday of American Liberalism 1945–1968* (Cornell University Press, 1998), pp. 157–162.

73. A recommended source for information about this rebellion is Dan Georgakas and Marvin Surkin, *Detroit: I Do Mind Dying: A Study in Urban Revolution* (South End Press, 1999) (also http://libcom.org/history/detroit-i-do-mind-dying-study-urban-revolution).

74. Thomas J. Sugrue, "On the Line: Blacks and Auto Work." (http://www.autolife.umd.umich.edu/Race/R_Casestudy/R_Casestudy5.htm#popsugrue)

75. "Japanese Workers, Their Companies and Society: Lifetime Employment, Perks and Changes" (http://factsanddetails.com/japan.php?catid=24&blogid=3&subcatid=156). See also, Kazutoshi Koshiro, "Lifetime Employment in Japan: Three Models of the Concept," Foreign Labor Developments, US Bureau of Labor Statistics, August, 1984 (http://www.bls.gov/opub/mlr/1984/08/rpt4full.pdf).

76. Simon Mundy and Song Jung-a, "Strikes Reflect Shift in South Korea Politics," *Financial Times*, September 10, 2012 (http://www.ft.com/intl/cms/s/0/411fcc06-fb34-11e1-a983-00144feabdco.html).

77. Ben McGrath, "Big business demands lower wages in South Korea," World Socialist Web Site, May 20, 2013 (http://www.wsws.org/en/articles/2013/05/20/kore-m20.html).

78. Reuters, "GM to Discuss Labor Woes With South Korea President, Union Rep Says," *Automotive News Europe*, May 7, 2013 (http://europe.autonews.com/apps/pbcs.dll/article?AID=/20130507/ANE/130509909/gm-to-discuss-labor-woes-with-s-korea-president-union-rep-says).

79. "Auto Boom in Mexico Worries US Workers, Unions," *Macomb Daily*, July 18, 2013 (http://business-news.thestreet.com/the-macomb-daily/story/auto-boom-mexico-worries-us-workers-unions-1/1).

80. See, for instance, America M. Kiddle and María L.O. Muñoz eds., *Populism in Twentieth Century Mexico: The Presidencies of Lázaro Cárdenas and Luis Echeverría* (University of Arizona Press, 2010); Steve Dubb, *Logics of Resistance: Globalization and Telephone Unionism in Mexico and British Columbia* (Routledge, 1999), p. 82; Jonathan C. Brown, "Labor and the State in the Mexican Oil Expropriation," Paper No. 90-10, (University of Texas at Austin, 1990).

81. Helen J. Muller, Robert R. Rehder, Geoffrey J. Bannister, "The Mexican-Japanese-US Model for Auto Assembly in Northern Mexico," *Latin American Business Review*, Vol. 1, No. 2, 1998 (http://www.unm.edu/~hmuller/hybridEDIT.htm).

82. Nick Miroff, "In Mexico, Auto Industry Fuels Middle Class," *Washington Post*, April 3, 2012 (http://articles.washingtonpost.com/2012-04-03/world/35450993_1_auto-industry-middle-class-auto-workers).

83. Edward Niedermeyer, "Is China's Cheap Labor A Thing of the Past?" *The Truth About Cars*, September 29, 2011 (http://www.thetruthaboutcars.com/2011/09/is-chinas-cheap-labor-a-thing-of-the-past).

84. Boy Luthje, "Auto Worker Strikes in China: What Did They Win?" *Labor Notes*, December 23, 2020 (http://www.labornotes.org/2010/12/auto-worker-strikes-china-what-did-they-win).

85. Lance Carter, "Auto Industry Strikes in China," *Insurgent Notes*, October 28, 2010 (http://insurgentnotes.com/2010/10/auto-industry-strikes-in-china).

86. Kerswell, op. cit. Kerswell uses these charts to prove how consistent the pay gap is between workers in the countries of the "global north" and "global south." He seems much less interested in the consistent differential between autoworkers and garment workers in each country.

PHOTO CREDITS

page 8 "Franklin D. Roosevelt," photographer unknown (source: U.S. National Archives and Records Administration).

page 14 "Spectrum-06-1," by Derek Blackadder (CC BY-SA 2.0).

page 15 "111117-D-BW835-016," Department of Defense by Erin A. Kirk-Cuomo (CC BY 2.0).

page 18 Library of Congress, photographer unknown.

page 26 "Travel: Zambia 5," by Bypassed tumblr (CC BY-NC 2.0).

page 30 "Egyptian workers march to Shura Council on May Day 2013," by Gigi Ibrahim (CC BY 2.0).

page 31 "Jakarta Mall, 2004," by Jonathan McIntosh.

page 34 "Jakarta Mall," by Jonathan McIntosh.

page 40 "Call center jobs pay $1,600 - $8,000/year," by Marc Smith (CC BY-SA 2.0).

page 42 "'Namaste, one zero eight': Inside india's first domestic emergency call center, 2007," by David Robinson (CC BY-SA 2.0).

page 44 "Workers at Garfield," by CTA web (CC BY-ND 2.0).

page 47 "Pickets, Safeway, California, 1973: Filipino United Farm Workers Union (UFW) supporters picket outside of a California Safeway store," photographer unknown.

page 48 "César Chávez, speaking at a United Farm Workers rally, June 1974," by Joel Levine (CC BY).

page 51 "120507-N-SH505-005," by by Mass Communication Specialist Seaman Jasmine Sheard (US Navy).

page 54 "young_worker.JPG," by Maritime Union of New Zealand (CC BY 2.0).

page 55 "Workers Day of Action (7/24/2012): Unions, low-income workers, and supporters rally to demand better pay and working conditions, and increase in minimum wage," by Joe Lustri (CC BY 2.0).

page 58 Noam Chomsky at Jobs With Justice conference.

page 59 "Students and Workers Unite + Jeff Stone=Walker Clone," by marctasman (CC BY-SA 2.0).

page 61 "8 Hour Day Signs," by Harris & Ewing, Library of Congress Prints and Photographs LC-DIG-hec-07566.

page 63 "Free Labor Will Win," Office for Emergency Management. Office of War Information. Domestic Operations Branch. Bureau of Special Services. (03/09/1943 - 09/15/1945) National Archives.

page 64 left: Henry Ford, Library of Congress; right: "Autoworkers' houses. Flint, Michigan, 1937," by Dick Sheldon, Library of Congress Prints and Photographs LC-USF34-040024-D.

page 66 "Installing Body Wiring On The Cadillac Assembly Line," by Joe Clark (Environmental Protection Agency), in National Archives, Creative Commons.

page 68 "Assembly line at Hyundai Motor Company's car factory in Ulsan, South Korea, 2006," by Taneli Rajala. GNU Free Documentation License, Version 1.2.

page 71 Volkswagen de México, 2012, Creative Commons.

page 72 "Thank a farm worker! On March 5th 2011 a group of 50 YAYA members and supporters set out to Tampa, Fl to march and protest with the Coalition of Immokalee Workers in support of their Publix to "DO THE RIGHT THING" campaign," by National Farm Worker Ministry (CC BY 2.0).

page 76 "Construction Workers III," by Kevin Schoenmakers (CC BY-NC-ND 2.0).

**Exodus and Reconstruction
Working-Class Women at
the Heart of Globalization**

Bromma

ISBN: 9781894946421

Kersplebedeb 2012

34 pages • pamphlet • $4.00

Examining the decline of
traditional rural patriarchy,
and the centrality of
working-class women's
exploitation and resistance in
globalized capitalism:

"*Whatever radicals in the metropolis decide to do,
or not do, capitalism has moved on. Its current
incarnation demands the thorough commodification and
internationalization of agriculture, industry, commerce and
services. It needs rapid access to mobile and flexible pools
of workers, especially working-class women. To make this
happen, capitalists are rolling the dice, scrambling to extend
their domination even as they allow some of capitalism's
deepest social moorings to slip free. In desperation, under
duress, capitalism has found it necessary to socialize the
labor of working-class women on a whole new basis, to
essentially remake the working class in a more advanced
and cosmopolitan form. In the process, the central role of
working-class women in the world economy is being pushed
rapidly out of the shadows.*

"*New capitalism is here, bringing with it new politics. At
the most fundamental level, this politics is not about oil.
It's not about religion. It's not about imperialist men versus
anti-imperialist men. It's about women and women's labor:
women at the heart of a transformed global proletariat.*"

Amazon Nation or Aryan Nation

White Women and the Coming of Black Genocide

Bottomfish Blues

Kersplebedeb 2014
ISBN 9781894946551

168 page paperback

$12.95

The two main essays in this book come from the radical women's newspaper *Bottomfish Blues*, which was published in the late 1980s and early 90s, while an appendix on "The Ideas of Black Genocide in the Amerikkkan Mind" was written more recently, as one of a number of "post-Katrina" working papers. On their own or taken together, these three texts provide raw and vital lessons as to the intersections of nation, gender, and class, from a revolutionary and non-academic perspective.

Divided World Divided Class

Global Political Economy and the Stratification of Labour Under Capitalism

Zak Cope

Kersplebedeb 2012
ISBN 9781894946414

385 pages paperback

$20.00

This book demonstrates not only how redistribution of income derived from super-exploitation has allowed for the amelioration of class conflict in the wealthy capitalist countries, it also shows that the exorbitant "super-wage" paid to workers there has meant the disappearance of a domestic vehicle for socialism, an exploited working class. Rather, in its place is a deeply conservative metropolitan workforce committed to maintaining, and even extending, its privileged position through imperialism.

KER
SPL
EBE
DEB

Since 1998 Kersplebedeb has been an important source of radical literature and agit prop materials.

The project has a non-exclusive focus on anti-patriarchal and anti-imperialist politics, framed within an anticapitalist perspective. A special priority is given to writings regarding national liberation, anticolonialism, and armed struggle in the metropole; the continuing struggles of political prisoners and prisoners of war; and global political economy and crisis.

Kersplebedeb can be contacted at:

Kersplebedeb
CP 63560
CCCP Van Horne
Montreal, Quebec
Canada
H3W 3H8

email: info@kersplebedeb.com
web: www.kersplebedeb.com
           www.leftwingbooks.net

Kersplebedeb

Made in the USA
Monee, IL
03 December 2024

72069412R00056